Shell
Shell
Shell
63
M.SANDOZ
outils métal dur
M.SANDOZ
outils métal dur

PORSCHE 911 CARRERA

Chris Harvey

CONTENTS

Titles in the *Super Profile* series

Ferrari 250GTO (F308)

Jaguar Mk 2 Saloons (F307)

Lotus Elan (F330)

MGB (F305)

Morris Minor & 1000 (ohv) (F331)

Porsche 911 Carrera (F311)

Further titles in this series will be published at regular intervals. For information on new titles please contact your bookseller or write to the publisher.

ISBN 0 85429 311 6

A FOULIS Motoring Book

First published 1982

Published by:
Haynes Publishing Group
Sparkford, Yeovil,
Somerset BA22 7JJ

Distributed in USA by:
Haynes Publications Inc.
861 Lawrence Drive, Newbury
Park, California 91320, USA

Editor: Rod Grainger
Dust jacket design: Rowland Smith
Page layout: Mike King
Printed in England by: J.H.Haynes & Co. Ltd.

FOREWORD

Ten thousand feet up in the mountains of Mexico, the thin air was rent by an awful scream. The sound was harsh and metallic, like nothing else on earth, that of a 'primeval' Porsche racing car chasing glory in the Carrera Panamericana. It was the fifth and last of the great Mexican road races in 1954. When the sound and the fury had died, only the glory remained, and *that* name. It was the name, *Carrera,* which was to be borne over the years by the very best production Porsches, in memory of that great victory — a romantic name from a faraway place, symbolising the lure of the road. As their ancestry grew longer, new Carreras brought more and more glory to the firm from Stuttgart, until the greatest of them all was made in 1972. The 911 Carrera RS (for *Rennsport),* was the result of radical thinking and led to a new line of high-performance cars that re-established the 911 series in the forefront of Grand Touring cars. Not only have the 911 Carreras proved to be road burners without parallel, but surely the most versatile competition machines ever made, winning all manner of international events, both on the road and off the road.

It's always a pleasure to write about Porsches. You get to ride in such interesting cars and to meet such nice people. My special thanks to Josh Sadler and Steve Carr, of Autofarm, and to Allen Seymour, of Classic Car Valeting, for their help in the preparation of this book. My thanks also to the photographers and agency people who helped me provide the pictures: John Dunbar, Martin Elford and Kathy Ager of London Art-Technical, and my wife, Mary Harvey, of Hilton Press Services. Thanks, as always, to Chris Branston, Chairman of the Porsche Owners' Club of Great Britain, and to his executive director, Roy Gillham, and to Mike Cotton, of Porsche Cars (Great Britain) Ltd, for their enthusiastic support.

Chris Harvey

HISTORY

Not even the Porsche management realised what a success the Carrera RS would be when it was introduced in October 1972. The Chairman, Dr Ernst Fuhrmann, was keen on it: he saw the car as a way of swinging Porsche's policy on competition away from the almost ruinously-expensive turbocharged 917, that bore no outward resemblance to anything that could be driven on the road, towards production car racing and rallying. Porsche's salesmen, on the other hand, were against it: they knew that the firm had to produce at least 500 of the new cars a year to qualify — or to homologate — it for the international Group Four Special Grand Touring category, but they would have the task of selling these very specialised cars. Their arguments were reinforced by the contemporary trend in making sports and GT cars more luxurious — and, because the real purpose was to build an effective competition car, the 911 Carrera was anything but luxurious.

However, no matter how they tried, Porsche couldn't get the 911 homologated for saloon car racing — its back seats were simply not big enough. Therefore, Dr Fuhrmann gave the go-ahead for the 911 to be prepared for GT racing on a large scale. He helped the sales department by insisting that every eligible executive changed his personal transport to a Carrera.

Engineer Norbert Singer was given the task of finding out what was needed to put the 911 in the forefront of GT racing. Previous 911 competition cars — particularly the 911R (killed by the sales department in 1970) — had performed best at minimum weight. Taking the 911R, and the 911ST which succeeded it, as examples, Singer and his men reduced the new 911's weight dramatically by 200lb from that of the standard 911S high-performance model. This was achieved by using 0.7mm steel body panels rather than the normal ones of at least 1mm; fitting special lightweight Glaverbel windows, and making the engine lid from glass fibre. The well-padded interior of the 911S was replaced by simple trimming with no sound-deadening material, rubber mats rather than carpets, and lightweight competition seats in place of the normal thickly-upholstered squabs. The rear seats were dispensed with altogether, and so were such unnecessary items as interior door handles (replaced with a strap-operated latch), clock, passenger's sun visor, glovebox lid, and so on. A lot of weight was saved, too, by abandoning the normal thick sealing applied to the underside of the 911. A few more pounds (7.7 to be precise) was saved by using Bilstein, rather than Koni, shock absorbers.

Apart from these changes, the running gear of the Carrera RS was virtually standard. The suspension was strengthened by increasing the standard 15mm anti-roll bars to 18mm at the front, and 19mm at the back. Normal 911S 6-inch alloy front wheels were used with wider, 7-inch, rear wheels. These distinctive five-spoked wheels remained at 15 inches in diameter — a legacy of the days when the 911 was being designed in the early 1960s in which smaller road tyres could not cope with its performance. But new low-profile Pirelli CN36 radials with a 70 section at the front, and a 60 at the back, were fitted to give ultimate road-holding to the Carrera RS. This wheel/tyre combination gave the Carrera RS the greatest cornering power of any production Porsche of that time.

The rear wings bulged out gently to cover the new rear wheels, which had the added advantage of allowing even wider wheels to be fitted on pure racing versions. This was because the regulations said the width of homologated cars could be increased by two inches each side for racing. Other bodywork changes included moulding a distinctive 'duck's tail' spoiler into the engine lid to reduce lift and drag — and as a result to improve high-speed stability. Because the Carrera RS was intended primarily as a competition car, it was available at first only with the stiffest body, that of the fixed-head coupe.

The flat six-cylinder, all-alloy, air-cooled single overhead camshaft engine — the ancestry of which could be traced to Porsche's formula one car of 1961 — was a stretched version of the contemporary 2.4-litre 911S unit. It had the same 70.4mm stroke, but the largest bore that had been tried in a 911 engine: 90mm rather than the usual 84mm. This was achieved by using a technique perfected on the 917 racing cars (which shared the same bore and stroke although they had 12-cylinders). Experience with 2.5-litre short-stroke 911 racing engines had shown that they could not be bored out beyond 87.5mm without inviting trouble from the reduction in thickness of the Biral cylinder liners. Therefore an expensive, but hard-wearing, process developed for the 917 was used. This was a nickel-silicon carbide plating for the aluminium cylinders that needed only to be 1mm thick, enabling the bore to be increased beyond the limits imposed by the thick Biral inserts, within the restriction of the existing cylinder studs. This new Nikasil plating also reduced friction, and held oil well, enabling the engine to produce more power. Otherwise, the Carrera engine was similar to that of the 1972 911S, with the same fantastically-strong bottom end, chain-driven three-bearing camshafts, giant alloy cooling fan, and Bosch mechanical fuel-injection. The normal magnesium-cased five-speed all-synchromesh transmission was used in conjunction with the rear-mounted engine, although a stronger clutch spring had to be fitted to cope with the extra torque. Again, because this was essentially a competition car, the normal 911 option of Sportomatic semi-automatic transmission was not offered.

The torsion bar independent suspension was similar to that of the normal 911, with MacPherson struts and lower wishbones at the front, and trailing radius arms — called 'bananas' because of their shape — at the back, although the geometry had to be revised slightly to cope with the new wide wheels. Porsche retained their excellent rack and pinion steering and Ate disc brakes all round, with built-in drums at the back to give an efficient handbrake.

To help the sales people with their headache — as they complained that they could not sell the Carrera RS in their biggest market, America, because the new engine had not received emission approval — the price was held down to DM 33,000 (about £4,300 at that time) to promote sales in Europe. For an extra DM 2,500 (£325), however, a customer could have a touring package with full 911S interior and other fittings, such as steel over-riders.

These cars became known, retrospectively, either as the Carrera RSL (for RS lightweight), or as the Carrera RST (for RS touring). All these cars started life as lightweights to avoid trouble with the FIA over homologation: the FIA rightly suspecting that Porsche would dominate the GT categories as they had threatened to do with saloon car racing.

Imagine the surprise of the sales people — and, it had to be admitted, almost the entire staff of Porsche — when the 500 cars were all sold only a week after the model was launched at the Paris Salon! The demand continued, and the decision was taken to produce another 500, which meant that when they were complete — in April, 1973 — the Carrera RS qualified for Group Three GT racing, in which it had little opposition, and could run with few modifications. Throughout that model year, to the end of August, the Carrera RS production line kept going with 1,800 cars built in the 1972-73 F-series. Although they had their own batch of chassis numbers, they still carried the basic 911 code, with the next model year — from September 1973, to August, 1974 — being known as the G-series, and so on.

Initially, it had been possible to register these F-series cars, along with other series production 911s, individually through the local Stuttgart taxation office. The sharp-edged duck's tail spoiler would have given problems over legality had the car been presented in the normal way to Germany's national road licensing authorities. However, the Stuttgart taxation office could pass only 1,000 such vehicles and when Carrera RS production was in its later stages, many cars were produced without the spoiler, only to have them fitted as an accessory later by their owners!

Meanwhile, the Carrera RSR (for *Rennsport* racing) was developed from the lightweight base model RS. Between 50 and 60 Carrera RSs were taken from the assembly line and reworked in the customer service department. Their engines were modified with new cylinder liners and 92mm high-domed pistons to give a 10.5:1 compression ratio (instead of 8.5:1) with a capacity of 2,806cc. This was absolutely the largest bore possible in the existing magnesium crankcase. The cylinder heads were revised with extra-large valves and the cams modified to run in four bearings each. It was a tribute to the bottom end of the engine that it remained unaltered. These engines produced 300bhp against the normal 210, and were equipped with a large oil cooler in the centre of the front spoiler, with a smaller cooler for the transaxle under the off-side front wing. The braking system was uprated to 917 standards with cross-drilled discs, special calipers, and dual master cylinders linked by a balance bar. The widest possible wheels allowed by the regulations, with 9-inch front rims and 11-inch rear, were fitted with low-profile racing tyres. Special flared arches exactly two inches wider each side were fitted to cover these wheels. The suspension geometry and settings were revised to accommodate these new wheels and tyres. Later RSRs, based on the second series of 500 RSs, had further suspension setting revisions.

All manner of other permissible Group Four modifications were made, including fitting special fuel tanks, racing seats, roll cage, instruments and fire extinguishing system. Despite the price, nearly double that of an RS, these cars sold quickly because they were ready to race, rather than just a kit of parts as supplied by many other manufacturers.

The RSR had its first victory in the hands of Florida Porsche dealer, Peter Gregg, and fellow CanAm driver, Hurley Haywood, at Daytona in February 1973. The organisers had offered little starting money for the 24-hour event, so most of the sport racing prototypes stayed away. The four cars that did start broke down, leaving two RSRs — running as Group Five prototypes because they were not homologated in Group Four until the next month — to fight it out. Gregg's car finally beat the rival, driven by Mark Donohue and George Follmer, after a bitter battle.

Once they had qualified for Group Four, the RSRs ran away from the opposition, with the works entering two cars under Martini sponsorship. One of the Martini cars, usually driven by Herbert Muller and Gijs van Lennep, ran in Group Five with extensive modifications, including a new three-litre engine. The RSRs were so popular that they made up most of the field at Le Mans in 1973, Muller's Group Five car taking fourth place behind three other prototypes.

Another great victory occurred when Muller and van Lennep had outlasted all the other prototypes to win the last of the great open road races, the Targa Florio, with four other RSRs in the first ten. Clemens Schickentanz crowned a great season by sharing the European GT Championship with fellow RSR driver Claude Ballot-Lena. Gregg took both the TransAm and IMSA GT championships in America with his RSR against far more powerful Corvette and Camaro opposition.

Such was the versatility of the RS that it was also developed as a rally car, few major modifications being found to be necessary. The chief changes, other than in detail, were to the suspension rates and to the ride height. One of Dr Fuhrmann's special ambitions was to see a Porsche win the notoriously rough and difficult East African Safari Rally, so special models with 10 inches of ground clearance were built for use by Bjorn Waldegaard and Sobieslaw Zasada. These thrilling cars vied for the lead until Zasada overturned twice, and Waldegaard's car lost its oil cooler.

The Porsche factory could not devote a great deal of time or money to rallying, however, because they had far bigger things on their hands. It was the final year of the 917 in CanAm, and the entire 911 series had to be revised to enable the cars to withstand U.S. crash testing. In addition, the design of new models was underway to replace the 911s late in the 1970s — or at least that was the intention.

The G-series 911 was the car that many people said could not be made. Porsche bumpers had always been rather flimsy, especially those of the 911 built into the front and rear bodywork. It was difficult to see how they could be changed to meet the new U.S. regulations, which decreed that they should be able to withstand a 5mph impact (from a concrete block), without the lighting and other legal necessities being damaged. Most other manufacturers produced such weird and wonderful bumpers to meet this legislation that the appearance — and in some cases even the handling — of their cars was ruined, but Porsche managed with little apparent change! They simply reworked their bumpers in aluminium and mounted them on alloy struts running into the very strong floorpan. Hydraulic rams returned them to their original positions after impact!

Now that homologation had been achieved, the Carrera name was transferred to the top-line model in the standard road range. The 2.7-litre engine, with its mechanical fuel-injection and radical valve timing, was retained for the Carrera for markets other than the U.S. Cars bound for America were fitted with the 911S engine — now in 2.7-litre, rather than 2.4-litre, form — which had K-Jetronic electric fuel injection to meet emission regulations. This 'softer' engine produced 175bhp.

Transferring the name Carrera to the normal 911 range also meant that the standard model was now fully trimmed, fitted with electric windows, and was available with the option of a Targa top — that is an open body with a massive built-in roll cage. A new line in alloy wheels was also adopted.

For a time, the rear spoiler was not available on German Carreras because of the taxation office's objections, but before long a solution was found in the form of a new spoiler with rubber edges, which were also added to the front 'chin'. The interior of all cars was also revised to meet the new U.S. safety regulations.

The five-speed transmission was fitted as standard on European Carreras. American Carreras had a four-speed transmission as standard, with the fifth gear as an option, so that a cheaper model could be marketed for people who didn't feel it was necessary to change gear so much. People who sometimes didn't like changing gear at all could now order for their Carrera the Sportomatic semi-automatic gearbox formerly offered on lesser 911s.

The cost of all this development, and the expensive competition programme was starting to catch up with Porsche, however, and their cars were moving from the medium price range to those of the exotic, where most of the opposition had far larger engines. It was evident that more power had to be extracted if the 911 was to remain competitive in this market — and it would have to be done by methods other than dramatically enlarging an engine that had always given problems with so much weight behind the rear wheels.

So, much of the works development from this point was concentrated on turbocharging, with blown Carrera RSRs spearheading their campaign in 1974. These cars were far nearer to the next Porsche GT — the 930 — however, than the existing

Carrera, so they are not the subject of this book. The turbocharged cars suffered from an embarrassing amount of throttle lag, which meant that the 911 engine had to be reworked to give more torque. This was achieved by changing the cylinder stud spacing to allow a 95mm bore, giving almost a full three-litres (2,994cc).

The benefits of this engine, developed on the Group Five Carrera RSR in 1973, were carried over to the Group Four RSRs for 1974. It used a stronger aluminium block, and had throttle slides, rather than butterflies, for extra power. Group Three versions of this car took over the Carrera RS designation with 230bhp for the 1974 season. The new RSRs had 330 bhp.

They used 917 wheels — 10.5 inches wide at the front, and 15 inches at the rear — with the 917's titanium hubs, plus coil-spring reinforced suspension. They also featured the new 'picnic table' spoiler that was to make its appearance on road cars.

Porsche's involvement with GT and prototype racing was concentrated on the 911 when fuel consumption restrictions outlawed the 917/30 turbocharged car from CanAm. Porsche took third place in the World Sports Car Championship (behind ultra-light Matra and Gulf prototypes), with the Turbo RSR in 1974. Privately-entered Carrera RSR 3.0s abounded with the four leading cars split between two German teams run by Georg Loos and the Kremer brothers. Amazingly, they shared the same top driver — the Briton John Fitzpatrick — who won the European GT championship after switching backwards and forwards between the teams. Numerous other top-line drivers thrilled the crowds with very close racing in the RSRs, Gregg and Hayward winning the Watkins Glen six-hour GT class, and the Camel GT and TransAm Championships.

Waldegaard came close to winning the East African Safari on his second attempt with a 2.7-litre RS, but — much to the disappointment of the factory — a driveshaft broke when he was leading by miles. It happened during a tropical storm in the middle of the night, and it took hours to reach him — with the result that he had to settle for second place. Other RSs performed well in rallying, particularly in the hands of Irishmen Cahal Curley and Ronnie McCartney.

There were few changes to the Carrera's specification for the 1975 model year because Porsche were fully occupied with the 911 Turbo — called the 930 because it featured such extensive changes from the basic specification. In essence, it was an RSR with a very high standard of trim (in keeping with its equally high price tag) and the 3-litre turbocharged engine developed from that of the Turbo Carrera racers. It was a lot heavier than the earlier cars, however, which explains why the original Carrera RS was almost as fast and has since become such a classic with its nimble handling. Californian Carreras had to be fitted with even more stringent emission control equipment, which reduced their power to 165bhp, the other U.S. Porsches being known as "49-state cars." The Sportomatic transmission was modified to take advantage of the better torque band in the European Carrera, one of the four ratios being abandoned, and the other three strengthened.

The RSR 3.0 litre cars continued to make up the bulk of the fields in long-distance sports car racing in 1975, with Gregg and Haywood winning the Daytona 24-hour event before Gregg went on to win the Camel GT series from Haywood and Al Holbert. Gregg raced a long-tailed RSR 3.0 in two events — running as much as three seconds a lap faster than the opposition — before this variation, based on the shape of the CanAm 917/30, was outlawed. The chief opposition to the all-conquering Carreras came from works BMWs, with Chevrolet Monzas and Corvettes making up the rest of the American fields.

In Europe, the Loos RSRs again dominated Group Four races with the most consistent opposition from teams run by the Kremers, and the German Porsche dealers, Tebernum. Loos had the best drivers, however, in Fitzpatrick, Tim Schenken, Toine Hezemans, and Manfred Schurti, but they split events between themselves, allowing Tebernum star Hartwig Bertrams to win the European GT Championship on consistency. Fellow RSR driver Claude Haldi combined his racing with rallying and took enough points to win the coveted Porsche Cup for the best performer using a car of the marque. Le Mans was almost a Porsche procession, with seven RSRs following Fitzpatrick's car in fifth place!

In Group Three, the Carrera RS was virtually unbeatable, winning the European Hillclimb Championship for Jean-Claude Bering, and national rally championships throughout Europe. Porsche offered a Group Four racing version of the 930, the 934, to privateers when long-distance racing regulations were revised in 1976, but the normally-aspirated RSR 3.0 still continued to be popular, winning a number of events, especially when the turbos blew up.

Major changes were afoot with the production cars, too. The I-series machines, introduced for 1976, were especially significant in that they featured total galvanisation of the steel used in the chassis platform. Now that everything structural was made of galvanised steel of varying thicknesses, Porsche were able to give a six-year guarantee against underbody corrosion — a historic achievement that was unmatched at the time. The steel cost slightly more and there were a lot of problems with zinc fumes given off during welding, but the result was a considerable boost to marketing as the cars now enjoyed either a far higher resale value or simply lasted longer for those who wanted to hold on to them.

The standard Carrera was revised with an 8.5:1 compression ratio version of the 930's 3-litre engine. It was fitted with K-Jetronic fuel-injection so the valve gear had to be modified to suit its characteristics. In this form, the engine produced 200bhp, and this tamer version of the Carrera became known as the Carrera 3 in Europe and the 911S in America. It was during this year, also, that the 930 was called the Turbo Carrera in the U.S. The Carrera 3 (or 911S) was also offered with a Sport package that included the options of the 930's wide wheels, low-profile tyres and extended wheel arches. Cars bound for America could also be ordered with a Tempostat cruise control which would keep the car going at any chosen speed until it was cancelled either manually or by accelerating or braking. It could be reset instantly to its original reading by a lever. This device was controlled by pulses from an electronic speedometer and proved popular for long, boring, freeway journeys at the 55mph blanket speed limit.

Amazingly the old RSR 3.0 cars still remained competitive in top-line events in 1977, with one example driven by Haywood, John Graves and Dave Helmick winning at Daytona after Jochen Mass's works turbocharged Porsche 935 hit tyre problems. In rallying, Michele Mouton from France won the European Ladies' Championship with a Carrera RS, and in Rallycross private entrants such as John Greasley continued to campaign the RS to great effect.

Lots of small changes were made to the J-series cars for 1977, with one major new option — a "Comfort" pack for the American 911S, which was also available on the Carrera 3. This comprised softer Bilstein shock absorbers with 14-inch alloy wheels and Uniroyal Rallye 240 tyres. These options smoothed out the ride of the 911, but imposed a speed limitation of 130mph because of the tyres. As a result, cars with this package had a speed limiter in the distributor and markings on the speedometer at 130mph. They were inclined to wallow much more than the stiffer-sprung, larger-tyred, Carreras, and showed a tendency to oversteer.

The gearbox on manual cars, practically all Carreras, in fact, was modified to accommodate twin baulking segments in the first and second ratios, with revised first-gear cogs to ease engagement from neutral. The ventilation was also improved, which meant that it was possible to dispense with the quarterlights on the Targa. Porsches had been proving popular with thieves, too, so better locks were fitted.

In the following year, for the 1978 K-series, the engine was further detuned to give it more torque and the Carrera name was transferred to the new range of cars meant to replace the 911. The new 911 — which refused to lie down and die, selling just as well — became known as the 911SC.

Two of the new engines, as fitted to the 911SC, were uprated to 250bhp by fitting mechanical fuel-injection and the old type cylinder heads. They were then dropped into old-style Carrera RS bodyshells — complete with their nostalgic duck's tail spoilers — in a final attempt to win the Safari in 1978. Vic Preston and Waldegaard fought valiantly to give the 911 Carrera a glorious swansong, but their haul was yet another second place, and fourth. The Carrera spirit lives on, however, in competition versions of the 911SC, which have won the Monte Carlo Rally, while genuine old-style Carreras still mop-up scores of awards in the world's sporting events.

EVOLUTION

F & G-Series

The standard Porsche 911 Carrera was launched in fixed-head RS form on October 5, 1972. Its specification was similar to that of the basic 911's with a rear-mounted engine and transaxle unit, all independent torsion bar suspension, disc brakes all round, rack and pinion steering, and bodywork made chiefly from steel in unitary construction with a steel floorpan. A five-speed gearbox was fitted as standard with the 911 engine enlarged from 2.4-litres to 2.7. Mechanical fuel injection was used in conjunction with radical valve timing in the flat six-cylinder overhead cam air-cooled engine for maximum performance. Alloy wheels were fitted all round with the rear wings widened to cover 7-inch rims. The vast majority of Carrera RSs were built in left-hand-drive form for use in Europe, with a brief production run of about 100 in the right-hand-drive configuration for the British market. Most cars were fitted with the more luxurious 911S trim at the factory after assembly, in addition to comprehensive undersealing. They can still be distinguished from standard cars converted to RS specification, however, by their thinner metal body panels. These cars became known as the RS Touring (RST) models, with the original, lighter, competition machines subsequently called the RS Lightweight (RSL). Very few lightweight cars were made in the right-hand-drive form, although some Touring models have subsequently been converted as far as possible to this specification. The standard colour for most of them (until more than 1,000 had been made), was white with a choice of blue, red, or green wheel centres and matching side striping carrying *"Carrera"* lettering; this side decoration could be deleted as an option. Between 50 and 60 of the F-series Carrera RSLs were converted at the factory to the extensively-modified RSR specification.

In September 1973, the basic 911 was revised to meet U.S. safety regulations by fitting hydraulic ram bumpers. The Carrera became available with all the standard range's options, such as a Targa top. In fact, two Targa tops were available, one with a detachable plastic panel and a more expensive one with metal folding panels. The metal panel top was fitted as standard when air-conditioning was specified, because it needed less space in the luggage compartment. Electric windows were fitted as standard to the Carrera, and the duck's tail spoiler became optional. Later, during the G-series run, it was replaced as an option by a 'picnic table' spoiler with a rubber lip for the front air dam. The interior was revised to meet the new U.S. regulations, with black fittings replacing chrome. Chrome trim was still available for the exterior as an option. A single 12-volt battery replaced the twin 6-volt units. A 2.25-gallon screen wash reservoir was fitted in the nose. More rigid rear suspension arms were adopted with larger rear wheel bearings. A variety of anti-roll bars were offered to suit individual tastes in ride and handling. Non-U.S. Carreras were fitted with five-speed manual gearboxes and the RS engine as standard; U.S. ones had the option of four-speeds and were fitted with the less-powerful 911S engine, which had been uprated to the same capacity as the RS, but fitted with K-Jetronic electric fuel-injection. The gearlever on all cars was made less sensitive to accidental bumping, and a larger, 9.8-inch, brake pedal lever was fitted for extra leverage. Parts of the chassis were made from galvanised steel. New pattern alloy wheels were offered as an option. A total of 109 cars were converted at the factory to new RSR and RS specifications.

H-Series

The new alloy wheels became standard on the Carrera introduced in September 1974. The chief changes to the car were inspired by the new Turbo introduced for the 1975 model year. The heating system was revised with an integral fan and the option of an automatic sensor, and the alternator uprated to 980 watts at the same time. Sound insulation was improved with an electric sunroof offered as an option on fixed-head models. Other options included the Turbo's headlight-cleaning system. The top two ratios in the manual gearbox cars were raised for more relaxed cruising, and the Sportomatic gearbox revised as a three-speed to make operation smoother. The rubber lip was removed from the front spoiler and the duck's tail option dropped. Californian Carreras were fitted with additional anti-emission devices.

I-Series

The I-series cars introduced in September 1975 had the entire floorpan made from galvanised metal and were offered with a six-year guarantee against underbody corrosion. Sound-proofing was further improved at the same time as the floor pressings were redesigned. The Carrera was fitted with an 8.5:1 compression ratio version of the Turbo engine, taken to 2,994cc by enlarging the bore to 95mm. This involved making new cylinder blocks, which were now cast in aluminium. K-Jetronic fuel injection was fitted as standard, the new model being called the Carrera 3 in Europe and the 911S in America; the Turbo then took the name Turbo Carrera in the U.S. The Carrera 3, or 911S, could be ordered with a Sport package made up of wider Turbo wheels, tyres and arches. All models were fitted with a new five-blade cooling fan to allow higher revs for its integral alternator, thus boosting output. U.S. cars were given the option of having a Tempostat cruise control fitted.

J-Series

Lots of small improvements were made to the J-series for 1977. The gearbox on all manual cars was modified to accommodate twin baulking segments in the first and second ratios, with revised first gear cogs to ease engagement from neutral. The interior was uprated by fitting a new console to take cassette tapes — a far cry from the original Carrera! — and the Comfort package was offered on all 911s, although it seems doubtful that it was fitted to any Carrera.

SPECIFICATION

Type designation

Porsche Carrera RS, Carrera RSR, Carrera RSR 3.0, Carrera, or Carrera 3

Number built & chassis numbers

6834 built at Stuttgart-Zuffenhausen, Germany, between October 1972 and August 1977, chassis numbers: 9113600001-9113601036 (F-series fixed-head coupes); 9114600001-9114601036 (G-series fixed-head coupes); 9114610001-9114610433 (G-series Targa); 9114400001-9114400528 (G-series, US-specification, fixed-head coupes); 9115600001-9115600518 (H-series fixed-head coupes); 9115610001-9115610197 (H-series Targa); 9115400001-9115400395 (H-series, US-specification, fixed-head coupes); 9116600001-9116601093 (I-series fixed-head coupes); 9116610001-9116610479 (I-series Targa); 9117600001-9117601473 (J-series fixed-head coupes); 9117610001-9117610646 (J-series Targa).

Drive configuration

Rear-mounted engine, five-speed gearbox, rear-wheel-drive.

Engine

Flat six-cylinder, all alloy, single overhead camshafts, 2687cc, 90mmx70.4mm bore and stroke (Carrera RS and Carrera); 2806cc, 92mmx70.4mm bore and stroke (Carrera RSR); 2992cc, 95mmx70.4mm bore and stroke (Carrera RSR 3.0 and Carrera 3). Compression ratio 8.5:1 (Carrera RS, Carrera, Carrera 3); 10.5:1 (Carrera RSR); 9.8:1 (Carrera RS G-series). Maximum power 210bhp at 6300rpm (Carrera RS and Carrera); 175bhp at 5800rpm (Carrera, US-specification); 308bhp at 8000rpm (Carrera RSR); 315-330bhp at 8000rpm (Carrera RSR 3.0); 230bhp at 6200rpm (Carrera RS G-series); 200bhp at 6000rpm (Carrera 3). Maximum torque 188lb/ft at 5100rpm (Carrera RS and Carrera); 174lb/ft at 4000rpm (Carrera, US-specification); 217lb/ft at 6200rpm (Carrera RSR); 232lb/ft at 6200rpm (Carrera RSR 3.0); 203lb/ft at 5000rpm (Carrera RS G-series). Bosch mechanical fuel-injection on all models except the Carrera 3, which had K-Jetronic fuel-injection.

Transmission

Five-speed, ratios: 3.18, 1.83, 1.26, 0.96, 0.76, final drive 4.43, other ratios available (Carrera RS); 3.18, 1.83, 1.26, 0.93, 0.72, final drive 4.43, other ratios available (Carrera RS G-series and Carrera 3); numerous ratios optional (Carrera RSR, RSR 3.0).

Chassis

Steel floorpan, unitary construction with steel body, some glass fibre panels, particularly on the RSR. Wheelbase 2260.6mm/7ft 5in. Front track 1381.76mm/4ft 6.4in (Carrera RS, Carrera, Carrera 3); 1430.02mm/4ft 8.3in (Carrera 3 Sport); 1435.1mm/5ft 1.4in (Carrera RSR); Rear track 1394.46mm/4ft 6.9in (Carrera RS, Carrera, Carrera 3); 1465.58mm/4ft 9.7in (Carrera 3 Sport); 1663.7mm/5ft 10.4in (Carrera RSR). Overall length 4163mm/13ft 7.9in (F-series); 4291mm/14ft 1in (G to J-series). Width 1661.16mm/5ft 5.4in (Carrera RS, Carrera, Carrera 3); 1770.38mm/5ft 9.7in) (Carrera 3 Sport); 2118.36mm/6ft 11.4in (Carrera RSR). Height 1320.8mm/4ft 4in (Carrera RS, Carrera); 1272.54mm/4ft 2.1in (Carrera 3). Weight — ready to drive - 2388lb (Carrera RST); 2150lb (Carrera RSL); 2075lb (Carrera RSR); 1875lb (Carrera RSR 3.0); 2470lb (Carrera 3).

Suspension, wheels and tyres

Suspension (front) independent MacPherson telescopic damper struts, lower wishbones, longitudinal torsion bars, (rear) independent trailing radius arms, transverse torsion bars, telescopic dampers. Wheels 15in x 6in front, 15in x 7in rear (Carrera RS, Carrera, Carrera 3); 15in x 6in front, 15in x 8in rear (Carrera 3 Sport); 15in x 8in front, 15in x 9in rear (1973 Carrera RSR); 15in x 10.5in front, 15in x 15in rear (1974 Carrera RSR).

Steering and brakes

Rack and pinion steering. Disc brakes all round, cross-drilled on RSR.

Electrics

12-volt, two 36Ah batteries, 770watt alternator, Bosch distributor, two iodine headlamps (Carrera RS); Bosch electronic ignition one 12-volt battery (Carrera); Bosch electronic ignition, 980watt alternator (Carrera 3).

Performance (factory figures)

Max speed 152mph/245km/h, fuel consumption 16.2mpg (imp)/13.4mpg (US)/17.46 1 x 100km (Carrera RS); max speed 149mph/240km/h, fuel consumption 15.7mpg (imp)/13.1mpg (US)/18 1 x 100km (Carrera); max speed 178mph/286km/h, fuel consumption 6mpg (imp)/4.99mpg (US)/47 1 x 100km (Carrera RSR, average); max speed 143mph/230km/h, 18.2mpg (imp)/11.98mpg (US)/15.52 1 x 100km (Carrera 3). Acceleration (independent road tests) 0-60mph 5.5 secs, standing ¼-mile 14.1 secs (Carrera RST); 0-60mph 5.6 secs, standing ¼-mile 13.2 secs (Carrera RSR).

ROAD TESTS

AUTO TEST

PORSCHE CARRERA RS TOURING

Sensational, even by Porsche standards

AT-A-GLANCE: "Homologation special" which demand must make into a full production Porsche. Extraordinary performance, yet more tractable than other Porsches. Superb brakes, roadholding, traction and steering; but demands expert driving more than other cars of similar performance. A classic whose speed makes its price more justifiable than is usual.

Without any particularly dramatic announcement, Porsche quietly presented the Carrera RS to the public at last autumn's Paris Motor Show. Boring out the 2,341 c.c. six-cylinder *Boxermotor*—as the Germans have it—of the 911 series by 6 mm put the principal dimensions of the engine to 90×70.4 mm, the capacity up to 2,687 c.c., maximum power to 210 bhp (DIN) at 6,300 rpm, and peak torque to 188 lb ft at 5,100 rpm. Five hundred cars were to be made in order to qualify the car's entry into Group 4 sports-car racing. Every one was ordered before it was built. So far as any Porsche enthusiast is concerned, it is hard to see how the factory can avoid making as many Carreras as possible. It is the fastest road-going Porsche and also, perhaps even more valuably, the most tractable.

Differences

The Carrera RS Touring is based on the previously fastest similar Porsche, the 911S, and uses much of the 911S equipment and specification. To put the Carrera's statistics into perspective, the 911S engine has the same compression ratio (8.5-to-1), maximum power of 190 bhp (DIN) at 6,500 rpm, and peak torque of 159 lb ft at 5,200 rpm. Actual differences in engine construction are limited to more heavily ribbed cylinder barrels (15 instead of 11 cooling ribs)—these barrels cannot be re-bored, understandably—slightly flatter-topped pistons, and altered ignition timing. The Bosch fuel-injection pumps have a suitably uprated output. Crankshaft, camshafts, valves, cylinder heads and valve timing are 911S; like its predecessors of late, the RS runs happily on normal 2-star 91-octane fuel. The same 7/31 (4.429-to-1) final drive and five-speed gearbox are used, but 4th and 5th ratios are a little higher; the use of 215/60 VR 15 in. Pirelli Cinturato CN36 tyres on 7 in. rims at the rear puts the calculated overall gearing up to 24.06 mph per 1,000 rpm. At the front (and on the spare) 185/70 VR 15 in. tyres are used on 6 in. rims. The same hefty sized anti-roll bar (0.59 in.) is fitted front and rear (front only on the 911S), a lighter forged aluminium alloy front sub-frame is employed, dampers are Bilstein at both ends, and the rear suspension is reinforced. The most obvious external difference is the dolphin-like dorsal spoiler which is part of the glass-fibre engine cover; the ordinary engine cover is available if specially ordered, but Porsche point out that it is no gimmick, improving rear adhesion above 100 mph, improving straight stability and actually lowering the drag coefficient of the body. Independent confirmation of that last claim was supplied by a road test in a German magazine which found that, using the standard engine cover lowered the maximum speed by 4½ mph.

There are variations in specification; the car tested is the Porsche Carrera RS Touring (code-numbered M472); there is the Carrera RS itself (M471); a third variation is listed, the Carrera RS Racing version (M491). By the usual removal of items like soundproofing, electric windows and so on, a claimed 250 lb is removed on the Carrera RS which is usually known unofficially in this country as the "lightweight".

Handling experiments on a wet MIRA circuit. The lefthand bend was entered at about maximum speed for the conditions. Initially accelerating in the corner to tighten the effective cornering line by breaking away the tail only made the car run wide; traction and adhesion of the rear is too good for the front, which loses grip. Therefore, a moment before this point the throttle has been released, upsetting the car's balance, breaking away the back tyres; the driver must be quick to catch the resulting slide, which begins sharply. The wheel-lifting is not nearly as alarming as it looks. Although the MIRA track surface is a very good one, it says much for both the car and the Pirelli tyres (here on standard pressures) that there is enough grip in the wet to generate such cornering forces

Traction is outstandingly good; note the nose-up attitude under heavy acceleration on this wet surface

AUTOCAR 31 May 1973

Performance

As usual on current Porches, starting from cold is an uncharacteristically restrained business of lifting the rich mixture lever in between the seats, and turning over the engine, without any noticeable pressure on the organ accelerator pedal, whereupon the engine fires and slowly increases its tickover. Warming-up is very quick—one of the few advantages of the Porsche's engine-blown heater is felt here, in the very early delivery of heated air for demisting on a cold morning. With a warm power unit, starting is much more of an indication of what is to come—turn the key and the engine leaps into life with stirring alacrity, almost as if there is no flywheel at all—throttle response is more like a racing car than a roadgoing one. Press the clutch pedal, which needs a surprisingly low 30 lb effort, and engage first gear—the gearchange too is very light most of the time—and move off. One might expect to have to use high rpm and lots of clutchslip to get away. Nothing could be farther from the truth. More so than its smaller brothers, the Carrera will potter about contentedly for as long as you like, tick over reliably, and is appreciably more flexible than the others. We have a suspicion that it is also slightly quieter, though only a side-by-side test could decide the point.

So, you can drive out of built-up areas with no unseemly indication that you are in an unusual Porsche—apart perhaps, in the case of the test car, from the fin and heavy sign-writing along the sides. Get clear of restrictions and, for a beginning, put your foot down in, say, third gear; this gives you a little more time to appreciate exactly what happens.

Starting from below 20 mph, the car accelerates, but not excitingly. At 1,800 rpm it begins to pull acceptably, continuing unexceptionally to around 3,000 rpm. At 3,200 rpm the note of the always audible engine changes and the car shoots forward; at 4,500 a heartwarming deep growl begins and one feels an almost unbelievable further increase in the pressure of the seat on one's back which is vastly exhilarating, continuing as it does all the way to around 7,000 rpm. An ignition cut-out prevents one revving beyond 7,200 rpm, which is just as well, because the way the revs rise, especially in the lower gears, makes it all too easy to over-speed the engine.

At MIRA, the acceleration figures obtained were outstanding. After several experiments, we found that the clutch did not care for clutch-slipping starts; in an interesting mechanical example of being cruel to be kind, the safest way to get off the line was to rev to between 5,000 and 5,500 rpm, and to let the clutch in as if the pedal had suddenly become red-hot. Only then was it possible to break the exceptionally sure grip of the Cinturatos on the tarmac to produce wheelspin instead of clutchspin. Nevertheless, so quick was the car's getaway and so good its traction that the black marks continued for only a relatively short way. Once the wheels had gripped again, changing gear at around 6,750 rpm, one was in 1st for only a very short time; 2nd took one from 37 mph to 64 mph; 3rd to 93; 4th to 127; and a brief snatch of top gear just after 124 mph and the kilometre took the car to a clear 130 mph before we had to brake for the end of the straight. Times recorded on our electronic recorder confirmed the fact that this Porsche is one of the world's fastest roadgoing cars, at any rate at the more frequently used lower and middle ends of the speed scale. Thirty mph appeared in 2.1 sec; 50 in 4.6; 60 in 5.5; 80 in 9.6; the quarter-mile in 14.1; 100 in 15.0; 120 in 21.9; the kilometre in 25.4; and 130 in just over half a minute.

Aerodynamics lesson still visible half an hour after a wet motorway drive. Turbulence and what the makers say is an area of positive pressure deposits road filth behind the dorsal spoiler, in contrast to the relative cleanliness of the smoothly swept body in front and around the fin

We took it to Belgium for maximum speed runs where it recorded 149 mph both ways in good conditions. Unfortunately, we have not tested the 911S with the 2.4-litre engine, but the slightly better-than-specification 2.4 911E tested in *Autocar* of 25 November 1971 with 165 bhp at its disposal was 10 mph slower, got to 60 mph in 6.4 sec; the quarter-mile in 14.4; 100 in 17.2; and 120 in 1 sec longer than the Carrera took to reach 130. One knows, all current Porsches are quick, but the 2.7 car is appreciably quicker than the rest.

Perhaps the most valuable point about this performance is that, for all normal road-going purposes, so much of it is so easy to use. The gearchange is very good; it follows the Alfa Romeo pattern, with reverse opposite 5th, but unlike the Alfa it takes a little more learning for those unfamiliar with it, because not having the Alfa's spring-loading of the gearlever into one spot—neutral between 3rd and 4th—one is not at first quite so sure where one is sometimes. First and 2nd are a little remote from the driver; the nearest the beat-proof synchromesh comes to baulking is felt when a noticeably higher pressure is needed to complete a change; this happens so seldom that it takes one by surprise. Ratios are perfectly suited to the car.

Thanks to the increased flexibility, one is not gearchanging all the time on a give-and-take road. Properly used, the thrilling reserves of power make overtaking wonderfully quick and safe; one is on the wrong side of the road for the shortest possible time.

Another major reason for the readiness with which one uses the performance is found in the superb way the car puts all the power down on the road. No wasteful, attention—getting wheelspin and attendant slewing; it simply *goes*—and how. Leaving a slow corner is one of the greatest and most satisfying pleasures of Carrera driving. You can "put the boot in" that little bit earlier on the exit, the car rocketing up the straight with the back wheels apparently glued to the road. Obviously, one has to respect the risk of breaking away the back end in such circumstances in the wet, but it is still remarkable how little twitch there is and how much acceleration—provided you don't abruptly alter your right foot.

If one were to establish a comparative factor of maximum speed divided by size of a car's body, the Carrera RS would, so far as we know, lead the road-going list. It is only 13 ft 8 in. long and 5 ft $3\frac{1}{2}$ in. wide; compare that with the $14\frac{1}{2}$ ft and $5\frac{3}{4}$ ft of the Ferrari Daytona, or the 15 ft and 6 ft of the Aston Martin V8. The point about this comparison is that such relatively small overall size—and especially the width—make it so much easier to drive the Porsche quickly on many British roads (where it is safe to do so, of course).

As before, our fuel-flow meter is not compatible with fuel injection, and no figures are obtainable from the manufacturer, so that we are unable to publish any steady-speed fuel consumption table. Overall we recorded 16.7 mpg, slightly better than the 15.6 mpg returned by the 911E Road Test car. For reasons that will be understood by foregoing remarks, during its 2,600 odd miles with us, the Carrera

Rear accommodation is minimal for people and quite handy for extra luggage when the "seat" backs are folded down

AUTOTEST PORSCHE CARRERA RS TOURING . . .

rarely was driven by any staff member with much thought to economy; consumption varied mostly between 15 and 18 mpg, though we did once see 20 mpg. Considering the performance—you could describe it as at least 4½-litres' worth from 2.7—such a thirst seems moderate. The test car had the ordinary 911S 13.6-gallon tank, which gave a restricted range at the high cruising speeds—120 mph—of which the car is capable; an 85-litre (18.7 gallons) plastic tank is available in Germany, but such tanks are not yet permitted in Britain. Some petrol pump attendants are sceptical about such a car running on 2-star fuel, and need reassurance.

Noise

The engine is dominant, as usual, when one is driving hard—the customary Porsche flat-six thrash that growls marvellously at mid-range as already described, rising to a unique, fairly subdued near-scream at the top end. Occasionally the test car disgraced itself with a loud backfire on the over-run. Gently driven, engine noise takes second place to the quite high level of bump-thump-induced road-roar that is generated over coarse concrete surfaces. We noticed some heterodying between 3,500 and 4,500 rpm. On a long journey one grows tired of the continuous drone behind. A slight increase in engine noise is noticed when the heater is turned to "hot". The transmission is often audible, clattering a little when pulling from low engine speeds, and also whining somewhat in all gears. There is some wind noise, mainly from around the front pillars, plus a little from behind.

Handling, ride and brakes

With only 41.2 per cent of the unladen weight on the front wheels, it is not surprising that the Carrera's steering is unusually light. Like all the rear-engined Porches it is a very relaxing car to manoeuvre for this reason. Possibly more so than the others, steering effort is directly proportional to cornering speed. As you corner faster, so the straightening pull on the steering wheel rim increases. There is, by other cars' standards, an unusually large amount of kick-back over any sort of unevenness. Correspondingly, feel is very good, assisted by the virtual lack of any stickiness or excess friction. Gearing is just right, 3.2 turns from lock to lock corresponding to a quite compact mean turning circle of 33½ ft diameter; the car is very swerveable, as any sports-car should be.

Straight line stability in still air even at maximum speed is good provided that the surface is smooth. On an uneven road there is a little wander, and side winds affect the car's progress a lot.

Steering load going up markedly with cornering speed, plus the combination of a lightly loaded front end, extremely good traction, and the great power of the engine combine to disguise to some extent the rear-heaviness of the car. Too much power in a bend merely increases the understeer induced by acceleration very noticeably. The best way to drive the Porsche round corners on public roads is also the only safe way in any case; assuming one can see and that all is clear, enter the bend no faster than is reasonable, begin to apply power in it, and then make the best use of the traction on the exit to accelerate away to great effect. Too early with the right foot does not often break the tail away except in slippery going, but merely makes the nose run wide. "Slow in, fast out" is the maxim.

So good is the roadholding of the Carrera RS on these remarkable Pirelli tyres in both dry and wet that very high cross-country averages can be achieved easily. The one and only catch remains. By sensible development—notably the replacement of the original very skittish swinging-axle rear suspension with a semi-trailing arm set up—the inherent dangers of the unavoidably imbalanced rear-engine design are largely avoided. The point at which a driver will run into difficulties is pushed so high that, for all normal purposes, the car is perfectly safe. But if, for whatever reason, a driver finds himself attempting a corner at too high a speed, and if he obeys his first instincts, which will probably be to decelerate, then the rear tyres can lose their grip so abruptly that it is difficult to hold the car out of a spin. Track experiments at MIRA revealed that, just before this point was reached, what felt to the driver like more than usual roll was partly the result of the inside front wheel lifting. Ride is appreciably better at high speed than at low, when it reacts quite sharply to some bumps. The usual rear-engine pitch is hardly present at all.

The brakes are superb, neither too light nor too heavy, which is remarkable nowadays when one sees that, as before, this latest Porsche still manages without any servo assistance. The pad material is a little dead at first, becoming more responsive as it is warmed; fade resistance is good. If one does have to brake really hard, it is comforting to know that the combination of rear-heaviness and beautiful braking balance is on your side; we achieved a best stop of just over 1g without any difficulty at all.

Engine room looks rather crowded at first sight. Note the various plates giving service information

Driving position

Few will quarrel with most aspects of Porsche interior design. The seat is very nearly as good as a rally-type for holding one in place, and can be adjusted to suit both short and tall drivers. The 911 body is a refreshingly good example of an uncommon quality amongst very fast cars today; it has good vision all round with no stupid styling blind-spots caused by heavy quarter panels. The windscreen wipers sweep an area of glass that suits right-hand-drive as well as left; they are as usual driven by a three-speed motor that gives 44, 64 or 86 sweeps per minute (we still think that it would be more useful to replace the slowest speed with a hesitation-wipe setting). The electric four-jet washers give floods of water just when you need it; their control is combined in a good stalk on the column. The rear screen has a two-position heater element; one can clear either the top two-thirds or all of the glass. As explained earlier, there isn't too much Porsche, so that although one cannot see both ends, one has a pretty good idea where they are. One can see about 3 in. of the fin in the inside mirror, but it doesn't block any vision that is needed.

Pedals are well-arranged, providing good heel-and-toe facility; the action of the throttle pedal is beautifully contrived, which is as it should be with such an engine. On a motorway, one finds it best to rest the unoccupied left foot between clutch and brake, since there isn't enough room to the left of the clutch. The hand-brake works well and is handy. So are all other important minor controls, the horn perhaps a little too much so; it is easy to sound it unintentionally.

Instruments are as on the 911S, from left to right, a fuel *and* oil contents gauge, oil temperature and pressure, 8,000 rpm revcounter, speedometer with trip, and a clock with a journey-start line on it. Manufacturers always seem to be glad to provide speedometers that, to the ignorant, suggest a top speed far higher than the car will actually do; this Porsche must be the most modest car ever in this respect, having a maximum reading only 1 mph (0.67 per cent) higher than its true maximum speed. The revcounter is bang in front of the driver and can easily be read; the speedometer on the other hand is obscured between 70 to 130 mph by the steering wheel rim.

Ventilation is good, but the heated-air heating system with its engine-fan-induced blowing is almost impossible to control easily and is responsible for some amusing effects. One succeeds in adjusting the temperature suitably at a steady speed on a motorway by mixing cold air with the electric blower. Then you leave the motorway; as you slow down, you lose heated air without losing cold air, so a wave of cold air comes in. Then, as you accelerate away down the road, a great wave of hot air engulfs you as the revs go up; an almost animal trait.

Rear accommodation is strictly occasional of course; but as a two-seater the Porsche is very practical. The boot is deeper than its shallow-look appears; two people can stow all they need for a Continental trip in the nose. Subtle design of the lock makes opening the bootlid very easy, despite the fact that, for obvious reasons it must include a safety second catch. A somewhat loose-fitting carpet covers the battery, jack and the spare

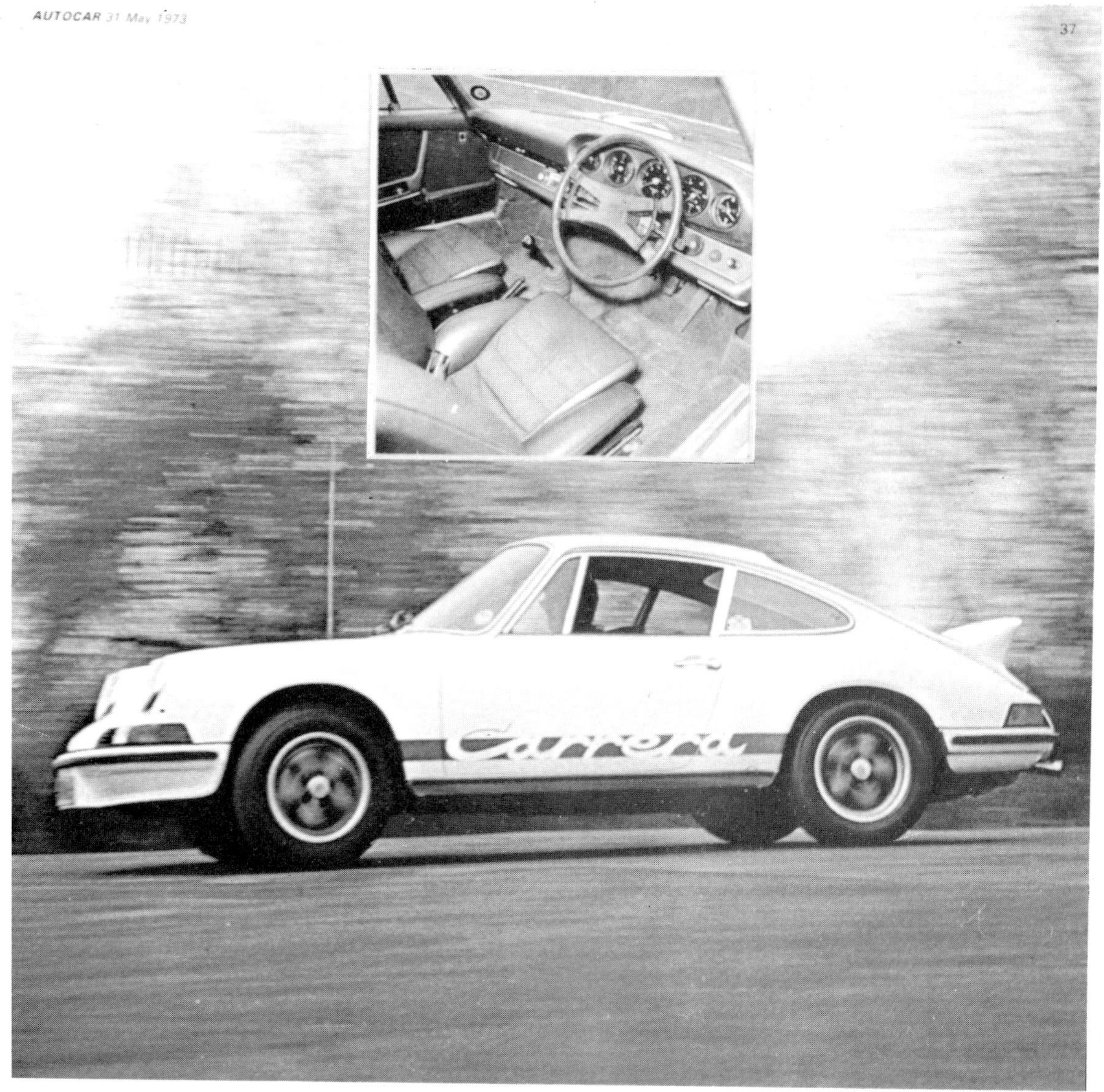

Signwriting on the side (in three colours to match wheels) is standard solely with this paint finish, called "Grand Prix White". It is not available with other finishes. MYX 4L is the car used to win the first round of the STP Championship for Production Sports-cars at Croft on 11 March (driven by Nick Faure). Only modifications for racing were the fitting of a roll cage inside, an external battery cut-off switch, full safety harness and two new rear tyres. Radio and aerial were left installed. Car was driven to and from the circuit (as, in some opinions, all production sports-car race competing cars ought to be)
Inset: Business-like dashboard is standard 911S

wheel. The bootlid release inside the car was a little stiff however on the test car. If necessary one can treat the space behind the front seats as upholstered luggage accommodation. In front there is a small locker, quite useful, and footwell pockets best used for maps.

A good driving mirror is fitted ahead of the front door. The quartz-iodine Bosch headlamps are very good indeed, giving a most reassuring spread and range of light on full beam without depriving one too badly on dip.

Living with the Carrera

Most of *Autocar*'s staff would be tempted to add, almost involuntarily after that heading, "Can't imagine anything nicer". Assuming you can afford it, the Carrera would be a very welcome companion, provided that you respected it as necessary. Being in group 7, sordid realities like insurance are a matter for discussion between the prospective owner and his broker. Most of the extras one would wish for are standard, such as electric windows. The test car came with a Radiomobile cartridge player-cum-wireless with electric aerial (£117), but without a limited slip differential (£94) or an electric sunroof (£178). Delivered in London the Carrera RS Touring adds up to £6,791.

Being such a clean shape, the car does not get filthy so easily as others do, except in the markedly turbulent area behind the rear spoiler, which becomes very grubby in sharp contrast to the swept lines of road filth on the smooth quarters to each side of the spoiler. Incidentally, it is important to close the engine cover by pushing down on the lip of the spoiler rather than on the back of the cover; it was pointed out to us how previous users, unaware of this, had caused the back of the cover to crack slightly.

The tool kit is excellent; five double open-ended spanners, one double-ended ring, one double-ended screwdriver, pliers, Allen key and a spare belt. Several examples of consideration for the owner are evident in the engine compartment. Metal plates carry various pieces of information, such as tyre pressures, how to check the oil level—which is done with the engine running

AUTOCAR 31 May 1973

PORSCHE CARRERA RS TOURING (2,687 c.c.)

TOTAL AS TESTED ON THE ROAD £7,349.90

ACCELERATION

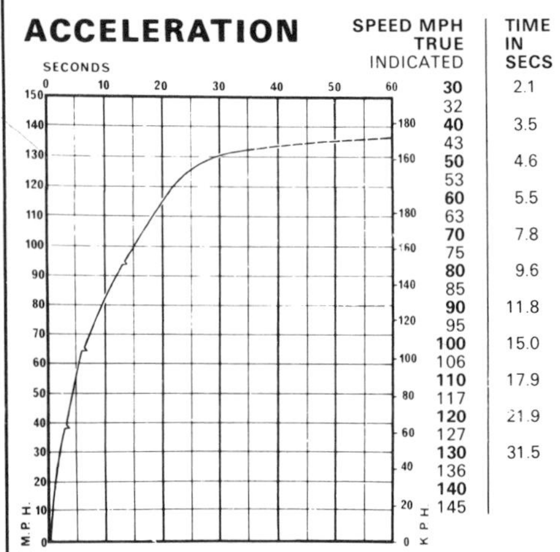

SPEED MPH TRUE	INDICATED	TIME IN SECS
30	32	2.1
40	43	3.5
50	53	4.6
60	63	5.5
70	75	7.8
80	85	9.6
90	95	11.8
100	106	15.0
110	117	17.9
120	127	21.9
130	136	31.5
140	145	

GEAR RATIOS AND TIME IN SEC

mph	Top (3.21)	4th (4.10)	3rd (5.58)	2nd (8.12)
10-30	—	—	—	3.0
20-40	—	—	4.2	2.3
30-50	—	5.6	3.3	2.0
40-60	8.0	5.1	3.0	2.1
50-70	7.8	5.0	3.1	—
60-80	6.7	4.6	3.2	—
70-90	7.8	4.6	3.8	—
80-100	8.3	5.4	—	—
90-110	8.7	6.4	—	—
100-120	9.7	8.1	—	—

Standing ¼-mile
14.1 sec 97 mph
Standing Kilometre
25.4 sec 124 mph
Test distance
1,380 miles
Mileage recorder
2.7 per cent over-reading

PERFORMANCE

MAXIMUM SPEED

Gear	mph	kph	rpm
Top (mean)	149	240	6,200
(best)	149	240	6,200
4th	136	219	7,200
3rd	99	160	7,200
2nd	68	110	7,200
1st	39	63	7,200

BRAKES

FADE
(from 70 mph in neutral)
Pedal load for 0.5 g stops in lb

1	45-40	6	40-35
2	45-40	7	40-35
3	40-35	8	40-35
4	40-35	9	40-35
5	40-35	10	40-35

RESPONSE
(from 30 mph in neutral)

Load	g	Distance
20 lb	0.22	137 ft
40 lb	0.42	72 ft
60 lb	0.64	47 ft
80 lb	0.85	35 ft
100 lb	1.03	29.2 ft
Handbrake	0.40	75 ft
Max. Gradient	1 in 3	

CLUTCH

Pedal 30 lb and 5¾ in.

COMPARISONS

MAXIMUM SPEED MPH

Ferrari 365 GTB/4 Daytona	(£10,347)	174
Lamborghini Miura P400S	(No longer available)	172
Aston Martin V8	(£8,827)	162
De Tomaso Pantera	(£6,604)	159
Porsche Carrera RS Touring	**(£7,193)**	**149**

0-60 MPH, SEC

Ferrari 365 GTB/4 Daytona	5.4
Porsche Carrera RS Touring	5.5
Aston Martin V8	6.0
De Tomaso Pantera	6.2
Lamborghini Miura P400S	6.7

STANDING ¼-MILE, SEC

Ferrari 365 GTB/4 Daytona	13.7
Porsche Carrera RS Touring	14.1
Aston Martin V8	14.1
De Tomaso Pantera	14.4
Lamborghini Miura P400S	14.5

OVERALL MPG

Porsche Carrera RS Touring	16.7
Lamborghini Miura P400S	13.4
De Tomaso Pantera	13.0
Ferrari 365 GTB/4 Daytona	12.4
Aston Martin V8	12.2

GEARING

(with 215/60 VR 15 in. tyres)

Top	24.06 mph per 1,000 rpm
4th	18.84 mph per 1,000 rpm
3rd	13.81 mph per 1,000 rpm
2nd	9.50 mph per 1,000 rpm
1st	5.476 mph per 1,000 rpm

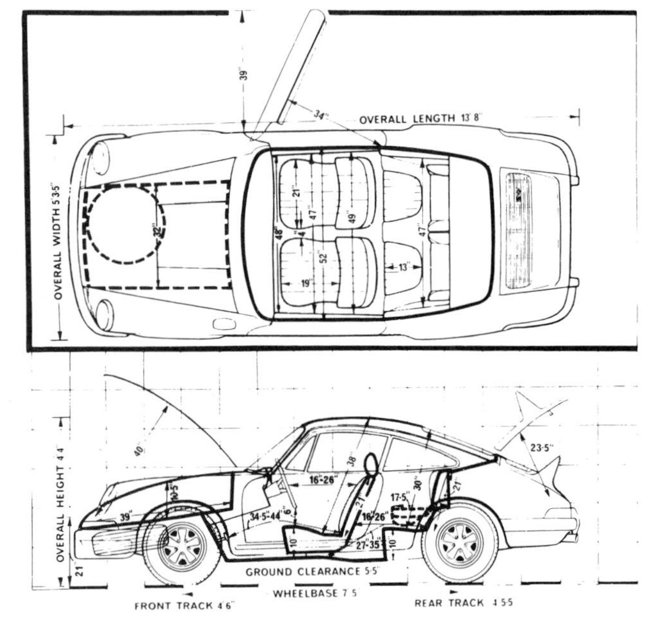

Standard Garage 16 ft × 8 ft 6 in.

CONSUMPTION

FUEL
Fuel injection system incompatible with *Autocar* flowmeter test system

Typical mpg 17 (16.6 litres/100 km)
Calculated (DIN) mpg (factory figure) 26 (10.8 litres/100 km)
Overall mpg 16.7 (16.9 litres/100 km)
Grade of fuel
Normal, 2-star (min. 91 RM)

OIL
Consumption (SAE 30)
600 miles per pint

TEST CONDITIONS
Weather: Dry. Wind: 8-12 mph.
(No wind for maximum speed runs.)
Temperature: 5 deg. C. (41 deg. F.).
Barometer: 29.2 in. hg. Humidity: 70 per cent.
Surfaces: Dry concrete and asphalt.

WEIGHT:
Kerb Weight 21.4 cwt (2,398 lb—1,088 kg) with oil, water and half full fuel tank).
Distribution, per cent F, 41.2; R, 58.8.
Laden as tested: 23.9 cwt (2,682 lb—1,216 kg).

TURNING CIRCLES:
Between kerbs L, 33 ft 3 in.; R, 33 ft 10 in.
Between walls L, 34 ft 7 in.; R, 35 ft 2 in.
Steering wheel turns, lock to lock 3.2.
Figures taken at 8,900 miles by our own staff at the Motor Industry Research Association proving ground at Nuneaton and on the Continent.

SPECIFICATION REAR ENGINE, REAR-WHEEL DRIVE

ENGINE

Cylinders	6, horizontally opposed
Main bearings	8
Cooling system	Ducted air, fan-forced
Bore	90.0 mm (3.54 in.)
Stroke	70.4 mm (2.77 in.)
Displacement	2,687 c.c. (163.9 cu. in.)
Valve gear	Single OHC per bank, finger-type rockers
Compression ratio	8.5-to-1. Min. octane rating: 91 RM
Carburettors	Bosch mechanical fuel injection
Fuel pump	Bosch electric low pressure mechanical high pressure, recirculating system
Oil filter	Purolator full flow
Max. power	210 bhp (DIN) at 6,300 rpm
Max. torque	188 lb ft (DIN) at 5,100 rpm

TRANSMISSION

Clutch type	Fichtel and Sachs, diaphragm spring, single dry plate, 8.9 in. dia.
Gearbox	5-speed all synchromesh
Gear ratios	Top 0.724 Fourth 0.925 Third 1.261 Second 1.834 First 3.182 Reverse 3.325
Final drive	Spiral bevel, 4.429-to-1

CHASSIS and BODY

Construction	Integral, with steel body

SUSPENSION

Front	Independent, longitudinal torsion bars, double wishbones, Bilstein telescopic dampers, anti-roll bar
Rear	Independent, transverse torsion bars, semi-trailing arms, Bilstein dampers anti-roll bar

STEERING

Type	ZF rack and pinion
Wheel dia	15.0 in.

BRAKES

Make and type	Dunlop-ATE ventilated discs front and rear, separate handbrake drum in rear discs, no handbrake
Servo	
Dimensions	F 11.1 in. dia R 11.4 in. dia
Swept area	F 235. in., R 208 sq. in. Total 443 sq. in. (370 sq. in./ton laden)

WHEELS

Type	Porsche forged aluminium alloy, 5-stud fixing 6 and 7 in. wide rims front and rear
Tyres—make	Pirelli
—type	Cinturato CN36 radial ply tubed
—size	215/60 VR 15 in.

EQUIPMENT

Battery	Two 12 Volt 36 Ah
Alternator	Motorola 64-amp a.c.
Headlamps	Bosch tungsten-halogen 120/110 watt (total)
Reversing lamp	Standard
Electric fuses	21
Screen wipers	3-speed
Screen washer	Standard electric, four-jet
Interior heater	Standard air-blending, type, engine-blower
Heated backlight	Standard two-stage
Safety belts	Standard
Interior trim	Pvc/cloth seats, pvc headlining
Floor covering	Carpet
Jack	Pillar type
Jacking points	One each side under sill
Windscreen	Laminated
Underbody protection	Galvanised main sub frame with pvc underseal and Tectyl treatment

MAINTENANCE

Fuel tank	13.6 Imp. gallons (62 litres)
Oil tank	17.5 pints (10.0 litres) SAE 30. Change oil every 6,000 miles. Change filter every 6,000 miles.
Gearbox and final drive	5.3 pints SAE 90. Change every 12,000 miles
Grease	No points
Valve clearance	Inlet 0.004 in. (hot) Exhaust 0.004 in. (hot)
Contact breaker	0.013 in. gap; 38° deg. dwell
Ignition timing	0° deg. BTDC at 900 rpm 32–38° BTDC (stroboscopic at 6,000 rpm)
Spark plug	Type: Bosch W265P21. Gap 0.022 in.
Compression pressure	Not available from manufacturer
Tyre pressures	F 28.5; R 28.2 psi (all conditions)
Max. payload	700 lb (325 kg)

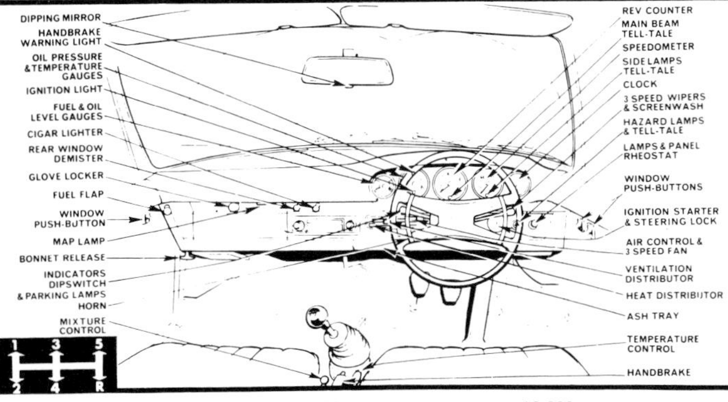

Service Interval	6,000	12,000
Time allowed	1.90 hours	7.00 hours
Cost @ £2.50 per hour	£4.75	£17.50
Oil	£1.90	£2.80
Oil filter	£2.51	£2.51
Breather filter	—	—
Air filter	—	£2.95
Contact breaker points	—	£0.54
Sparking plugs	—	£13.20
Total cost:	£9.16	£39.50

Routine Replacements	Time	Cost	Spares	TOTAL:
Brake pads	1.00	£2.50	£12.71	£15.21
Exhaust system	0.75	£1.90	£72.61	£74.51
Clutch	3	£7.50	£27.62	£35.12 ex.
Dampers—front pair	1.90	£4.75	£80.90	£84.65
Dampers—rear pair	0.50	£1.25	£37.34	£38.59
Replace drive shaft, (one)	1.00	£2.50	£57.59	£60.09
Generator	0.60	£1.50	£29.59	£31.09 ex.
Starter	0.70	£1.75	£58.09	£59.84

Boot lid is opened by means of the very easily worked safety latch. Luggage space is good for this sort of car. Spare wheel lives under the carpet and is a normal front size. Toolkit is excellent

since it is a dry-sump system; what the difference is between maximum and minimum on the dipstick; valve clearance (this is done with a neat diagram); maximum weights and the usual reference numbers.

Once one has learnt what to take notice of and what to ignore, the oil contents gauge is worth having. It does however give a pessimistic view of the oil level, which is best checked with the dipstick. Porsche apparently continue to insist that the owner uses a relatively "straight" engine oil; the car accordingly came to us with a gallon of Shell Rotella oil in the boot, of which its consumption was fairly frugal, depending on how hard one drove.

Accessibility, so far as the average owner will want access to this engine, is reasonably good. The throttle linkage is a somewhat alarming-looking assembly of ball joints and push-pull rods. The distributor is tolerably within reach, the coil is easy, like the oil filter, and oil filling is no bother. As usual, we like the thoughtful provision of a flap to stop petrol pump attendants scratching bodywork round the filler in the left-side front wing. The extensive amount of rubber round the car is welcome too.

Summing up, besides being the fastest of a very fast range of super sports-cars, the Carrera RS is also the easiest Porsche to drive and the most exhilarating. That does not deny the fact that it is a car that needs more care than most high-performance cars; but we think the care would be well worth it. □

MANUFACTURER:
Dr. Ing. H. C. F. Porsche AG, Stuttgart-Zuffenhausen, West Germany.

UK CONCESSIONAIRES:
Porsche Cars Great Britain Ltd., Falcon Works, London Road, Isleworth, Middlesex.

PRICES:

Basic (including Car Tax and Import Duty)	£6,539.00
V.A.T.	£653.90
Total (in GB)	£7,192.90
Seat Belts	(Standard)
Licence	£25.00
Delivery charge (London)	£6.00
Number plates	£9.00
Total on the Road (exc. insurance)	**£7,232.90**
Insurance	Group 7

EXTRAS (inc. PT)

Limited slip	£94.00
Electric sunroof	£220.00
*Radiomobile 108 S/R two speaker and electric aerial.	£117.00

*Fitted to test car

The cream of the Carreras

Why do most traditional Porsche fans rate the lightweight 2.7 Carrera of 1973 the most exciting production 911? Gordon Bruce supplies the answers

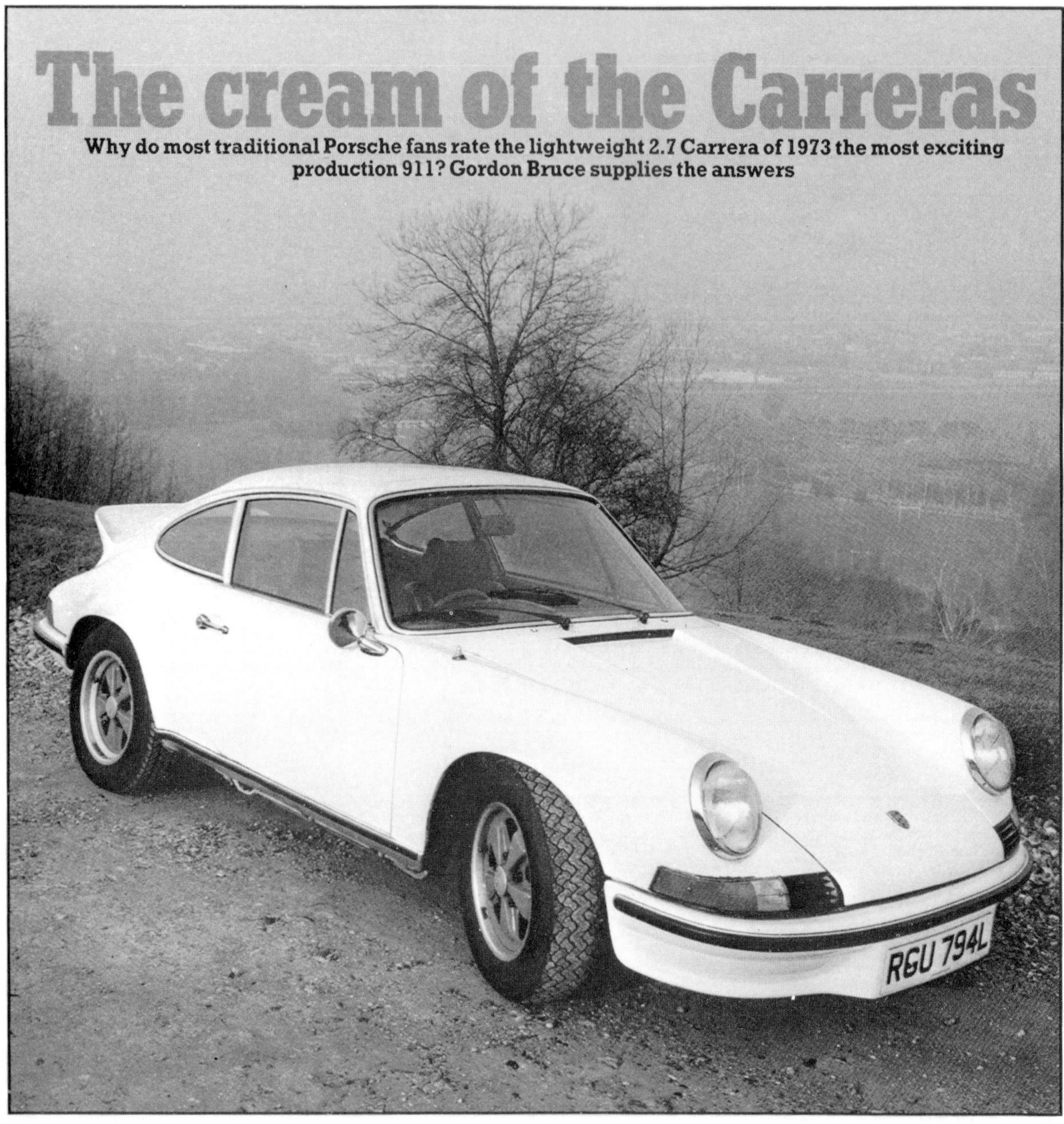

The success of Porsche's ubiquitous 911 seems to know no bounds. Now into its 18th year of production, it still has few if any peers on either road or track and if this year's Monte Carlo rally is anything to go by, even its career as a rally car is far from run.

Call it a triumph of development over design if you like, but age only seems to improve this, the most practical of all supercars. Certainly in terms of performance, economy, braking, ride and particularly handling the 911s of today bear little resemblance to their early ancestors.

That said, as is so often the case with a long line of motor cars, there is nevertheless one model that, regardless of age, stands out from the pack, that was ahead of its time, that offered an unmatched balance of all that separates the excellent from the exceptional. In the case of the 911 series, the superstar is without doubt the 2.7 Carrera RS of 1973.

The RS was born of Porsche's urgent need for something inherently quicker if their continuing supremacy on the race tracks was to be ensured. A true "homologation special", the Carrera RS was, in simple terms, a lightweight version of the 2.4-litre 911S with rear wings widened to accommodate 7ins wheel rims, a rear spoiler to reduce lift at speed and an increase in engine capacity from 2.4 to 2.7-litres.

Initially it was planned to build only 500 – the number required for entry into the Group 4 racing class. However, and not surprisingly so in hindsight, the car proved to be such an incredible success that no fewer than 1600 were made allowing entry to both groups 3 and 4.

Of those 1600, all started life as true lightweights but some 600 or so were sent back down the line for the addition of full 911S trim and equipment. The latter, the subject of this article, were designated Carrera RS Touring; rather less than 100 of which were imported in 1973. A few of the basic lightweights (RS) also crossed our shores, but they are both rare and very dear.

Despite the proliferation of "rogue" Porsches that now sport RS-type fins and arches it is still not too difficult to distinguish a real RS from its stablemates. Apart from the aforementioned extended rear arches, the salient points include the chin spoiler (as first seen on the previous year's 911S) and the highly distinctive rear 'ducktail' spoiler which is in fact just part of a complete glassfibre engine cover which served to combine improved aerodynamics with significant weight reduction. Colour is also a key factor in distinguishing these cars as the first 1046 were all finished in white; the owner being allowed to choose between blue, red and green as the contrasting colour for his wheel centres and Carrera side-flashes. In fact, the side-flashes, never the most subtle of decorations, were a delete option and many of the less extrovert owners opted to run without.

Surprisingly, the only significant change required to make the RS so much quicker than its predecessors was the increase in engine capacity from 2.4 to 2.7-litres. This was gained by employing a nickel-silicon carbide (Nikasil) coating for the aluminium cylinder walls and doing away with the previously used Biral cylinder inserts altogether; there having been insufficient 'meat' in the inserts to withstand further boring out. This change alone resulted in 10 per cent more power and no less than 18 per cent more torque to give 210bhp and 188lb ft respectively. No other notable changes were made to the specification, the major assemblies of this fuel-injected, dry sump, flat-six engine being well proven.

"Sensational even by Porsche standards" was the heading of the *Autocar* test on the RS Touring and how right they were, for it took Porsche themselves six years and the introduction of a turbocharged 3.3-litre engine to improve significantly upon the staggering performance figures of this 2.7-litre Carrera. With acceleration times of 0-60mph in 5.5secs and 0-100mph in 15.0secs, not to mention a mean top speed of 149mph, the RS was fast by any standards and will still show a clean pair of heels to today's 911SC let alone almost all other machines on the road.

'Sensational even by Porsche standards' . . . the 2.7-litre flat six gives 210bhp in the Carrera

Electrifying performance

However, there is a lot more to this 'hot shoe' than even its magnificent engine. It seems to be a fact of life that drivers either love or hate 911s – there is no half measure. Nevertheless, fan or foe, few who have been lucky enough to take the wheel of one, irrespective of the model, would disagree that the whole car seems to come alive to the touch of the controls. This phenomenon is particularly apparent in the RS. Quite how Porsche can make a 210bhp car of such electrifying performance yet endow it with perfect traffic manners is of course one of the best kept secrets of the marque. Rest assured that starting from hot or cold is virtually instantaneous and totally undramatic and that no amount of city slogging or traffic queuing seems to upset the status quo.

Temperamental it is not, but eager it most certainly is. Even while jostling for position on a suburban ring road you are left in no doubt of the calibre of machine at your command, so instantaneous is the throttle response, so agile the chassis. Then, at the sight of an open road, the Porsche somehow begs you to drop down through the gears and drive with a capital D – a true temptress at work!

That sharp throttle response is available anywhere in the wide rev-band (who said small, powerful engines have to be cammy?) but there are notable influxes of power at around 2000, 3250 and again at 4500rpm. At this point the already purposeful engine note switches to a nerve tingling growl as the driver is presented with a glorious rush of adrenalin pumping acceleration all the way to the (much needed) red line and accompanying ignition cut-out at 7200rpm. Change up and the orgasm starts again. And, if I tell you that using no more than 7000rpm you can reach 38mph in 1st, 67mph in 2nd, 97mph in 3rd and around 130mph in 4th you will appreciate why overtaking is not a problem in the Carrera!

The long-levered, five-speed gearbox is typical Porsche. Mistime your gearchanges and you are admonished by the synchromesh which promptly labours its movement. Get it altogether, as any self-respecting Porsche driver should, and the lever simply glides from ratio to ratio with the utmost satisfaction and as fast as you can properly co-ordinate the throttle and clutch.

Ah yes, the clutch. Like the brakes, this is operated by a pedal whose fulcrum is well below rather than above its centre point, the result is a slightly over-centre action which takes a little getting used to if smooth take-offs are to be the norm. Novice 911 pilots are not difficult to spot!

Talking of brakes, as befits a 150mph car, they are magnificent. Time and time again they will claw the machine down from unmentionable speeds without a hint of fade. Like every other aspect of the car, they inspire extreme confidence in the driver. A Carrera is a thoroughly engineered tool and very much up to the job in hand.

So to the handling and roadholding, always a subject for discussion where any 911 is concerned and one about which considerable rubbish has been voiced over the years. The general feel of the RS is obviously typical 911 with a tendency toward power-on understeer bred of a significant rearward weight bias. However, the "special tweaks" department has been at work on the suspension too, providing uprated Bilstein damping and stiffer anti-roll bars to complement the RS's wider rear track and increased power. The result is a car of rare qualities capable of breeding driver satisfaction in the extreme.

Sensitivity of handling

Sliding any Porsche under power is not a job for the faint-hearted yet nor is it the death-defying pastime some choose to believe. So taut is the RS chassis, so responsive the steering that every tiny movement of the car is relayed straight to the driver. Generally corners are best taken using the relatively light nose as a barometer of how quickly the power can be fed in at the exit – too much too soon and the nose will start to run wide. Certainly it is the car's almost unrivalled ability to sprint between the bends that makes Carrera motoring the thrilling pastime it is and the rare combination of sensitivity of handling and sheer brute power that makes it all possible.

Of course you can get into trouble if you try hard enough, the most likely way being to disturb the car's balance by lifting off in mid corner. Understandably, with so much weight biased to the rear, the tendency is for the tail to step out under such conditions and if it does you need to be reasonably rapid in winding on

Head down, owner Gordon Bruce enjoys the Porsche's superb combination of handling and power – it's a car of rare qualities capable of breeding driver satisfaction in the extreme

Carrera RS showing its colours – the rather garish and unsubtle outline side stripes were a delete option, the chin and engine spoilers signs of the real thing

the opposite lock. However, with experience, such techniques can be employed to real advantage and become a useful part of the Porsche driver's armoury. The rule is simple, tame the handling while reserving a degree of respect and you'll be king of the road. Treat the car with contempt and you'll be off the road!

German cars are not renowned for their plush interior and the RS is no exception in this respect. It is best described as very comfortable and highly functional. From the time you shut the close fitting doors, snuggle into the hip-hugging Recaro seats and grip the leather-covered wheel to when you dab the brakes for a 130mph curve you are aware of the inherent quality and of engineering bred of countless successes on the track. Everything you need is there where you would expect to find it; not least the magnificent group of instruments, the accuracy of which is abnormally high.

Appreciating asset

In terms of accommodation the car is really quite small and should be considered very much a two plus occasional (and preferably small) two rather than a four seater. Luggage accommodation, though better than it looks, is also limited yet there is plenty of storage space for odds and sods. 'Luxuries' inherited from the 911S and which distinguish the RS Touring from the bare RS include electric windows and a good measure of sound-deadening. There were also many factory-fitted options available such as an electric sun roof and limited slip differential. As can be seen, the RS Touring is an extremely civilised 'racer'.

Even the recession hasn't dampened the market for this particular collector's piece and it is one of the few apparently appreciating assets that really *is* appreciating. Examples in any condition are now highly sought and anybody who is lucky enough to have one in their stable should think very carefully before parting with it. Prices range from about £7000 for the really tatty ones to anything up to £15,000 for the mint ones. For some reason most seem to have covered around the same mileage and are currently displaying approximately 80,000 miles on their odometers.

Flight deck with the accent on the functional rather than the fashionable. The instruments are unusually accurate

Needless to say insurance companies are among the few who won't admire you for buying one and it's a good idea to check out the likely premium *before* signing on the dotted line. The good news is that earlier examples of Porsche, including the RS, do qualify for several of the classic car policies now available; which can be a very attractive proposition providing your annual mileage is relatively low.

In an era when even last year's cars can be dated by advancing technology, the Carrera RS stands head and shoulders above its competitors. Some may have more panache, some will be less dated in concept, but few if any will combine such effortless and usable reserves of performance with levels of braking and roadholding that could only stem from race-bred experience. If you want a car to pose in, then the engineering of this Porsche is wasted on you. If you want an appreciating asset that will out-perform almost every other car on the road and continue to do so long after its rivals have succumbed to wear and tear, then the Carrera RS could be the car for you. It's not so much a question of whether the car is good enough for you as whether you are good enough for the car!

The Carreras were so successful in production sports races – this is John de Stefano and Nick Faure at Oulton Park in 1973 – they were regarded as not playing the game

AUTOCAR, w/e 24 January 1976

TEST EXTRA

Porsche Carrera 3.0 Sportomatic

Carrera in 3 litre form has same power as superceded model but more torque. Sportomatic gearbox now with three speeds not four as before. Surprisingly acceptable in semi-automatic form though lacking the ultimate performance of the manual equivalent — economy little worse than manual car. Superb standard of interior and exterior finish. Now with 6-year corrosion-free guarantee on body base unit. Very expensive but almost unique roadholding, ride, performance and economy

IN the subheading of the *Autocar* Road Test of the Porsche Turbo, the phrase "total sophistication of an unpromising layout" was used in the context of the overhung rear engine arrangement. With typical thoroughness, Porsche engineers have grappled progressively with its shortcomings and have succeeded in overcoming practically all of them. Thus it should be no surprise that their solution to the problem of an automatic Porsche is just as thorough. It matters not that few people will want such a car, the point is that, if they do, then the Sportomatic gearbox offers perhaps an ideal answer. One might ask why Porsche bothered to produce an automatic gearbox at all and one must look across the Atlantic to the United States for the answer to that. Sales of the Sportomatic versions of the 911 and 912 models have been high there, aided no doubt by the American belief that a "stick shift" is youth-orientated, and so offering only four or five-speed manual gearboxes might narrow the demand for the model.

The appeal of the automatic gearbox in Europe and specifically in the UK is mostly to those drivers who spend a lot of time either driving in traffic or on motorways where no gearchanging is required. This should not be taken to mean that good cross-country performance is not obtainable for, even in its current 3-speed version, the Sportomatic gearchange only takes the edge off the performance, it does not dull it completely. As the performance figures reveal, the Sportomatic Carrera 3.0 remains a very quick car by any standard; but it lacks the ability of a 5-speed gearbox of providing the right gear at all times. Here we are talking of ultimate performance; for most needs the torque of the Carrera engine in 3-litre form is good enough to provide more than adequate performance.

For reasons of clarity, the Sportomatic gearbox has been referred to so far as "automatic" but it would be accurate to refer to it as "semi-automatic" instead, as it lacks "automatic" up or down gearchanges. Instead the driver must change gear with the gear lever which moves in a pattern similar to that for a normal manual gearbox. If the gearlever is left in, say, 2nd gear, then it will stay in that gear, the torque convertor multiplying the torque at the bottom end and the engine's rev limiter providing a stop at the top end. As in the previous 4-speed Sportomatic gearbox which was available up to the 3.0 litre 1976 model introduction, maximum torque convertor ratio is 2-to-1 and there is noticeable converter slip until the engine is revving at at least 3,000 rpm in any gear (equivalent to 25, 40 and 60 mph in the gears). Full acceleration is therefore not available until these speeds are reached. Thus, if the gearlever is left in top gear, there is a lot of slip taking place when driving around town — it can be done but it does mean that the throttle must be opened far wider than is necessary, with a consequent heavy penalty in fuel consumption.

It is much more satisfactory to

A happy absorption of 5mph bumpers and the discreetest of side-striping are familiar Porsche features. This is the non-Sport version of the Carrera without the aerodynamic aids first introduced on the 2.7 litre Carrera

Porsche Carrera 3.0 Sportomatic

use the gearbox like a manual one, the only unfamiliar aspect of which is that there is no clutch to depress. Unlike a fully automatic gearbox, the throttle must be closed as each gearchange is made. De-clutching of the drive occurs whenever the gear lever is touched, via pressure-sensitive switches at the base of the lever which operate the vacuum-actuated clutch. Thus it is vital not to keep hold of the gear lever after a gearchange and equally vital that the lever is not grasped in anticipation of a change. If it is an unconscious tendency of a driver to hold the gear lever, the Sportomatic is surely the very best means of breaking the habit.

Left: The familiar Porsche facia is dominated by the accurate rev counter. The left hand dial contains fuel and dry sump oil tank contents gauges. Just visible to the left of the steering wheel is the control lever for the Tempostat speed-hold device which has a memory to allow a selected speed to be retained

When climbing into the Porsche Sportomatic for the first time, only the full width brake pedal and absence of a clutch appear at all remarkable. The only other clue is that the gear lever knob has only three gear positions marked on it and also a "P" for Park to the top left position in the five-position gate.

Having described what Sportomatic is and a little of how it works, the next stage is to explain what it feels like on the road. What it does is to give the car a dual personality. If you are not in a hurry, and unlikely to need fierce acceleration, you can just engage top gear and only change down if the speed drops under about 20 mph. Where you are then scoring over the orthodox gearbox is that its 4th and 5th gears are so high that you cannot comfortably drop to so low a speed without needing a down change. But if you decide to hurry in more traditional Porsche fashion, you can change down and let the engine rev into the area where there is no torque convertor slip and where all the considerable power can be felt. This can be seen by reference to the acceleration in each gear which shows, for instance, that the acceleration from 50 to 70 mph in 2nd gear is no less than 1 sec quicker than that from 30 to 50 mph. You feel this on the road as a steadily increasing push in the back that does not tail off in 2nd gear from 10 mph all the way through to 90 mph.

Gearchanges can be made as quickly as the hand can move and, in fact, it is even more necessary to move the hand quickly in the Sportomatic because all the time it is on the gear lever, the clutch is disengaged. The only additional point that should be made about the gearchange is that it is best to engage 1st gear while still on the move; if it is engaged when the car is stationary, there is a distinct jerk. There is a tendency to "creep" at tickover and thus either the foot or handbrake are definitely needed to hold the car when at rest.

So much for the gearbox, what of the rest of the car?

Following policy set some years ago, AFN Limited as concessionaires for Porsche in this country import those extras suitable for the prestige end of the market and include them in the basic price. Thus such items as electric windows, opening rear quarterlights and the heated, servo-motor-driven exterior mirror are all included in the specification, as is an electric sunroof, Tempostat speed hold device, a rear window wiper/-washer and 5 mph recoil bumpers. The extras available on each model in the current range differ from car to car and those referred to are for the Carrera 3.0, in non-Sport specification. The Sportomatic gearbox is available as an alternative to the normal 5-speed gearbox at no extra cost. Thus for the car tested, the only options which could be specified are wheels with 7in. front and 8in. rear rim diameter, Recaro Sports seats and Bilstein shock absorbers.

The standard specification now includes a revised heating control system that we first tried on the Porsche Turbo. This system eliminates almost entirely the tiresome old Porsche shortcoming of temperature differences in the incoming air related to increases in engine speed. With the new system, a temperature sensor at the top of the windscreen gives information to a heating control system. If the temperature inside the car falls below that dialled by the driver on the convenient button between the seats, air is admitted to return the temperature to that requested. The system is a great improvement on previous Porsche systems although it is a little insensitive and the facia controls need to be juggled to give the right mix of heated and cool air.

In common with all 1976 specification models, the Carrera 3.0 has some minor revisions to the specification to improve road-holding. These evidence themselves in improved reaction to a mid-corner lift off the accelerator, there being

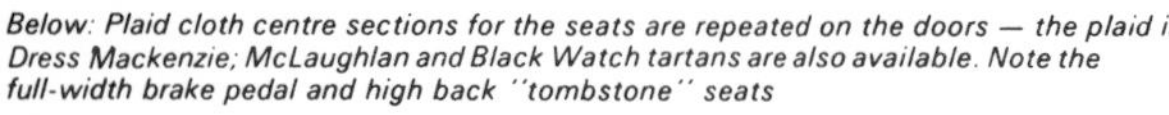

Below: Plaid cloth centre sections for the seats are repeated on the doors — the plaid is Dress Mackenzie; McLaughlan and Black Watch tartans are also available. Note the full-width brake pedal and high back "tombstone" seats

Below: With the back up, the rear seats take a child comfortably or an adult sitting crosswise. There are strap loops for luggage retention on the parcel shelf. The "T"-lever in the door jamb opens the engine bay cover

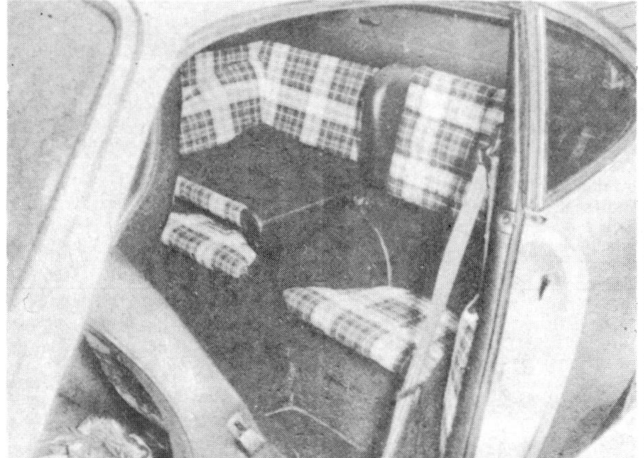

Left: Much air trunking and piping hide the fuel injection 200 bhp engine in its current 3.0 litre form. Access is good to items needful of routine maintenance, poor to others

Below left: The button in the door rail is the control for adjustment of the door mirror. The switches below the button are the controls for the electric windows

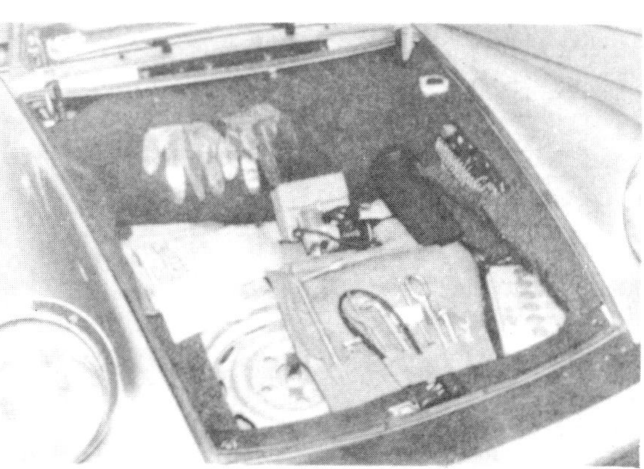

Below right: Ready access to battery, fuses and brake reservoir and the comprehensive toolkit. The compressor is for the Spacesaver tyre which in theory it would be illegal to use — Porsche supply a steel wheel and radial spare tyre with all new cars

less tendency to move towards terminal oversteer, and like the Turbo, the Carrera 3.0 can now be rated as a very safe sports car indeed — provided nothing really silly is attempted. The non-Sport version of the Carrera does not have the tail spoiler of the 2.7 litre car and this was noticeable at speed in crosswinds when the directional stability was not as good, though that is not to say that it was bad in this respect.

All the familiar messages of the road surface are still transmitted faithfully back to the driver by the quick, light steering that is such a likeable feature of Porsche cars. Corners are negotiated apparently by thought transference, only the lightest of pressure being required on the steering wheel. As ever, the ride is firm without being harsh, though especially at low speeds, major road irregularities cause the car to move rather abruptly. At higher speeds, the ride evens out and, provided that the steering wheel is not held too tightly, the car follows a reassuringly straight line, even over camber changes, brows and dips. With quite amazing adhesion available from the Pirelli tyres on wet or dry roads, and the absence of sudden torque reversals that automatic transmission confers, all the power can be applied at will as the traction is very good. Out of roundabouts or right angle junctions, the driver just needs to steer the car without need for special caution and in this respect, the car is most reassuring.

Though lacking "bite," the brakes are very powerful and despite the rearward weight bias, there is no tendency for the front wheels to lock under heavy application on wet roads. One usually associates automatic transmission with up-market cars that can be expected to have servo assistance for their brakes and the lack of it on the Porsche means that pedal efforts are high, made the more so by the disadvantageous pedal angle that results from floor-hinged pedals. Since the torque convertor makes engine braking less than would be the case with a normal gearbox/clutch arrangement, the brakes are used more with the Sportomatic and the heavy pedal efforts are rather wearing, especially in city centre driving. The brake pedal is full width and thus either right or left foot braking can be used.

Few cars have polarized opinion amongst the test staff as much as the Porsche Sportomatic. At first sight, the combination of the responsive and powerful fuel injection engine with the automatic gearbox seems an ill-judged exercise. After all, it is part of sports car thinking that the car should give the driver as much help in extracting the car's full performance potential as possible, and if this means that a 5-speed gearbox is required, then the Porsche one is as good as any. Is it sensible then, to provide only three gears and a lessening of control that inevitably accompanies the Sportomatic?

Opinions differed widely, those who only drive Porsches infrequently considering that the Sportomatic version was not a success and out of character. Those with the fortune to drive Porsches often felt that, with familiarity, the semi-automatic car could give performance approaching that of its manual stablemates and that, in some ways, the added relaxation enabled the car's other good points to be appreciated more. Such features as the low level of wind noise, the complete absence of body or suspension creaks and the low level of engine noise seem able to be more consciously valued. It is a fact that sales of the Sportomatic version are higher than one might expect and it could be that, in these days of restricted speeds, higher traffic densities and resentment towards very high performance, the Sportomatic version of the Carrera provides an acceptable compromise between performance and relaxed driving. It is the Jekyll and Hyde character of the car that allows it to fit the driver's mood so well — one minute threading its unobtrusive way through traffic, the next exploding away towards the horizon with that unmistakable Porsche exhaust note streaming out behind.

Maximum Speeds

Gear	mph	kph	rpm
Top (mean)	141	227	6,100
(best)	141	227	6,100
2nd	103	166	6,900
1st	61	98	6,900

Acceleration

True mph	Time secs	Speedo mph
30	3.5	30
40	4.8	40
50	5.9	50
60	7.3	60
70	10.0	70
80	12.4	80
90	15.0	90
100	18.5	101
110	25.7	111
120	32.7	122

Standing ¼-mile: 15.9 sec 93 mph
Standing kilo: 28.6 sec 115 mph

mph	Top	2nd	1st
10-30	5.5	3.8	2.4
20-40	6.0	4.4	2.5
30-50	6.9	5.0	2.3
40-60	8.4	4.5	2.7
50-70	9.9	4.0	—
60-80	10.2	4.3	—
70-90	9.5	4.9	—
80-100	9.5	6.4	—
90-110	11.1	— —	
100-120	14.1	— —	

Consumption

Overall mpg: 21 mpg (13.5 litres/100km).

Specification

Engine: 6-cyl horizontally opposed dohc, 95 x 70.4mm, 2956 c.c., compression ratio 8.5 to 1, Bosch continuous injection fuel injection; max power 200 bhp (DIN) at 6,000 rpm, max torque 182 lb ft at 4,200 rpm.
Transmission: Rear engine, rear wheel drive, 3-speed semi-automatic gearbox with vacuum-actuated clutch and Fichtel and Sachs torque convertor; gear ratios 8.1, 4.82, 3.12 final drive ratio 3.375 to 1. Top gear mph/1000 rpm 23.1. Suspension: Front independent MacPherson struts, lower wishbones, longitudinal torsion bars, anti-roll bar. Rear independent, semi-trailing arms, transverse torsion bars, anti-roll bar, telescopic dampers.
Brakes: Internally ventilated discs for all four wheels, 11.3 in dia front, 11.6 in dia rear. Dual hydraulic circuit.
Dimensions: Wheelbase 7ft 5½in; front track 54in, rear track 55in, overall length 14ft 1in; overall width 5ft 5in; height 4ft 4in; ground clearance 5in; turning circle 35ft 2in; unladen weight 22.1 cwt.
Other details: Tyres 185/70 VR 15 front, 215/60 VR 15 rear; fuel 17.6 gal (2-star); major service interval 12,000 mile; warranty 12 months, unlimited mileage; maximum payload 716 lb; boot capacity 9.8 cu ft.

OWNER'S VIEW

Josh Sadler and Steve Car, partners in the Porsche specialist firm of Autofarm, at Amersham, Bucks, have owned numerous Carreras and had three lightweights at the time they were interviewed by Chris Harvey . . .

C.H. Why are you so interested in the Carrera?
J.S. and S.C. Because it's about the same age as Autofarm! Our love affairs with Porsches started soon after we acquired and rebuilt a 911 when we both worked at a bearing company. *(Josh was a development engineer and Steve a test driver).* The Carrera was soon to become the ultimate 911, and we feel that we have grown up with it . . . so much so that we have three RS lightweights at the moment, in varying stages of rebuilding, including the very first one!
C.H. When and why did you buy that original RS lightweight, and what condition was it in?
J.S. and S.C. We bought it three years ago because it was like a dream come true. But it had had a hard life in rallying and it needs a complete rebuild. Although we buy and sell all sorts of Porsches, as well as repairing and renovating them, I don't think we would ever part with Carrera Number One.
C.H. Is it more economical to buy a Carrera in good condition, or in bad condition, and then rebuild it?
J.S. and S.C. Of course it's best to buy one in as good a condition as possible if you want to save yourself a lot of time and worry. But there's hardly anything, short of a corroded rear torsion bar tube, that's really terminal if the floorpan is not badly bent. It's also a lot cheaper and easier to build a competition Carrera than a road one because you don't need all the trim and the same standard of finish — such as door fitting — and so on. It's not necessary to use brand-new parts if you can't afford them — providing the parts under consideration are in good, sound, condition. Almost everything is interchangeable on 911s from the earliest made in 1964 to the latest 930s. The main problem with the Carrera when building one from the remains of another 911 is getting the suspension mounting points in the right place. We do it on a jig . . . but there's not many of those around.
C.H. Have you experienced difficulty in obtaining any parts?
J.S. and S.C. That's a loaded question! The basic answer, from the customer's point of view, is No. Practically everything for a Carrera is available, assuming that the enthusiastic owner can afford the parts. That's why, in company with similar firms on the Continent and in America, we specialise in replica parts as well as new. Really it all depends on what you want to do with a Porsche. To build a Carrera, you need parts from basically the same vintage, or later, as it is not worth bothering with some of the earlier parts, which were for far smaller engines. And it is not worth converting a Targa into a fixed-head coupe. It can be done with a lot of welding, but it's cheaper to sell the Targa and buy a fixed-head. If you want a really nice original Carrera, it is far better to replace the parts with new ones of original quality if the intrinsic value is to be preserved. Incidentally, many of the factory parts are now made in galvanised metal, which makes them better than new, and we doubt whether many purists really mind!

Porsche are remarkably good at supplying parts for the 911, but because they are produced in short runs their overheads are high and that is why they can be expensive — prices can also be boosted by the relative strength of the German currency and, in some cases, import duty. The procedures Porsche recommend, like their cars, are uncompromising in quality, and often expensive as a result. With the right experience, or advice, there are lots of corners that can be cut. You can, for instance, use a reconditioning kit of new parts to restore an old unit rather than replace the entire assembly.

Also there are so many unstressed panels in a Porsche, that it is worth considering glass fibre replacement parts because they are lighter, they don't rust, and they can cost only a fraction of the price of steel originals. We have our own glass fibre panels made to a very high specification by outside contractors and find ourselves exporting most of them to Germany!

There's such a demand for Porsche parts — from people keeping old Carreras on the road and from others building new ones — that it's worth specialists, such as ourselves, having them made if the factory parts work out too expensive. So nobody should go short of a part for a Carrera.
C.H. What kind of performance and handling does the car have?
J.S. and S.C. Out of this world! The RS lightweight really represents the pinnacle of 911 development for the road. That's why they are the classic of classics. If you like the handling of a rear-engined Porsche, there's none better than the Carrera, and there's hardly anything faster — certainly not from point-to-point. [And it's hard to think of anything

so quick on the road as the Sadler 3.5 Carrera].

C.H. Have your cars won any prizes in concours or in similar events?

J.S. and S.C. Certainly the cars we look after have been concours winners, but our personal leanings are more towards competition and the creative engineering that goes with it. Our future market has to be in restorations — we don't sell new cars — together with normal servicing. The only trouble is that restoring cars leaves very little room for creative engineering, and that's the side of the business that has given us the most satisfaction in the past. And then there's so much nonsense talked by some people seeking originality. I read somewhere recently that the first thousand or so Carreras off the production line were all white. Our Carrera number one is orange and always has been! [In the past Josh has specialised in hillclimbs — and National Championships — with trials and circuit racing as something of a sideline, and Steve in rallies and circuit racing.]

C.H. Is there an owners' club?

J.S. and S.C. There are few more enthusiastic clubs than the Porsche Owners' Club of Great Britain and similar organisations throughout the world. As enthusiastic club members, one of our pet projects at the moment is compiling a Carrera Register, with special interest in the lightweights.

C.H. What advice would you give the potential owners of Carreras?

J.S. and S.C. If you are in any doubt about the quality of a car, call in expert advice. Porsche bills can be very high, and the cost of a few hours' labour in a thorough inspection and test can pay untold dividends — and perhaps save the heartbreak of buying a car that you soon cannot afford to repair or run. And some things can be far cheaper to put right than you might think. This is because the engines and transmissions can be changed in a very short time on the 911 — so it can be nice to hear some good news on that front, too!

BUYING

The 911 Carrera is one of the few exotic cars that is really reliable, largely because of its magnificent engineering and the dedicated quality control shown by the factory. All Carreras had galvanised parts in their floorpans, to a larger or a smaller degree according to age. So the general rule is: the older the car, the more likely it is to show signs of corrosion. This applies particularly to the F-series RS with its extra-thin body panels, and even more so to the genuine lightweights which were not even undersealed. It is a pity because they are the most desirable of Careras for classic investment. On the credit side, there is little that cannot be rectified — often at considerable expense — on a Carrera, because the factory still run off batches of spare parts (including body panels), from time to time, and various specialists have their own made, often at a far cheaper price. The main problem with the Carrera is getting its suspension mountings in the right place if a substitute 911 floorpan is used in a rebuild.

Because of the basic similarity between all 911 Porsches, it is quite practical to use secondhand parts for restoration and running repairs, providing they are in good condition or can be repaired. This means that even the most derelict and damaged Carrera could be rebuilt — at a cost. Generally, however, the Targa models suffer far more than the fixed-heads from corrosion because their shells are more flexible. This causes seams to open up enough to let in the dreaded salt-water solution so prevalent on European and North American roads. Once it has penetrated the underseal, the rot sets in . . .

Bodywork Corrosion

The first points at which corrosion is likely to be found are all the usual ones associated with unitary construction cars. Road debris accumulates around the lighting units, wheel arches, wing tops, fuel filler flap box, front and rear shut faces, sills and doors. The front wings are relatively easy to replace because they are bolted on; the rear wings are more difficult because they are secured by welding. In common with all unitary-construction cars, the sills are vital structural members. They are made up of inner and outer sections, which are not expensive, but cost a lot to replace when labour is taken into consideration. On the Targas, the sheer weight of the engine and transmission can cause the body to sag if the sills are weak.

The roof of the coupe does an effective job of keeping everything together and seems to be rust-free! But if there is any suspicion about the quality of the doors' shut faces, it is essential to keep the seatbelts firmly secured, as the door catches can pull out of badly-corroded metal! The luggage boot lid, by contrast, usually presents few problems.

The steel engine lids are prone to rot and the rear centre panel, which carries the number plate light, is especially prone to rust. This is because of the continual changes in temperature in that area, caused by the proximity of the exhuast system, and the exposure to road debris and spray. This is also the cause of the Carrera's most common problem, that of corrosion in the exhaust systems's heat exchangers. Generally, they last only about two years. It is essential to replace them when they cause trouble, because, apart from affecting heating, prolonged use of damaged heat exchangers with mechanically-injected cars can lead to premature engine wear — the lack of heat keeps the automatic choke on, which, in any case, wastes a lot of fuel. Expensive engine trouble can also be caused by the original mild steel oil tanks — mounted inside the rear wings — corroding. Debris from rusty tanks gets into the engine and ruins the bearings. Corrosion can also start in the oil cooler, with similar results. A permanent cure can be affected to the oil tank by using a stainless steel replacement.

Mechanical

The most common problem is with the hydraulic timing chain tensioners. They are designed to work efficiently over the wide range of temperatures typical of air-cooled engines. This has the unfortunate effect of limiting their life to around 40,000 miles to 50,000 on average. The best way to test for such a condition is to run the engine at 2,500rpm in neutral and to listen for noises from the chain. They can often be quite violent, so they should not be missed. At higher revs, the tensioner tends to build up enough pressure to reduce the noise. Therefore, keeping the revs up is a way of limping home with such a problem, although immediate attention ought to be sought. The 2.7-litre cars with high-lift cams are the most susceptible to such trouble, because the tensioner has to work harder with them than in the 3-litre cars. The timing chain guides are made of rubber and can deteriorate in a similar way. As a result, oilways become blocked, leading the camshaft lubrication trouble.

The valve guides, particularly those for the exhaust, also wear, with 60,000 miles as the average life. The result is a smokey engine which burns a lot of oil, but replacements can be put off for a long while, providing the oil tank is kept well filled. Other items seem to start wearing badly at around 80,000 miles.

Collision damage

Apart from corrosion and wear associated with high mileages and age, it is essential to look for accident damage when considering the purchase of a used Carrera. This is because of the high degree of driving skill needed to conduct one to anywhere near the limits of its performance. The most obvious place to look at is any one of the four corners. The triangular strengthening member is often pushed back in a frontal impact, leaving a wavy floor, even after successful repairs. Such a floor need not necessarily adversely affect a car's performance if the rest of the car has been repaired properly, but it is a sign of what the machine has undergone. Door pillars can also be put out of alignment in a big crash, so check the gap around the doors. Marks on the window frames are also a good tell-tale sign of major impacts which have affected the doors. The most serious defect in a poorly-repaired car is likely to be misalignment of the track. Avoid such cars. The same strictures apply to the back of a Carrera, plus the common bending of the rear suspension's trailing arms as a result of hitting a wheel on a kerb or similar projection that might leave no other apparent mark. The later-style alloy wheels are far more likely to crack with such treatment than the earlier ones.

Summing-up . . .

From this catalogue of potential woes, it can be seen that the only way to repair a Carrera is properly, although it is quite practical to use second-hand parts from other 911s, providing they are in good condition. Without a doubt, the original RS is the most desirable model, particularly if it is in first-class condition, or the owner or purchaser is prepared to have the work done. The later cars are softer, more luxurious, machines still endowed with an incredible and quite useable performance. As a result, the almost macho Carrera RS commands the highest prices in perfect, original, condition, with the rest not far behind. With the G to J-series cars, the prices are largely dependent on age and condition. At present they vary from between a quarter to a half of the price of the average house in Britain, with dramatically lower values for specimens needing much work as this can be very expensive.

So far as buying a Carrera RS or RSR is concerned, the parameters are common to those which surround any used competition car: its history and originality are of paramount importance. Many of the early cars had a very rough life. They were rebuilt using all manner of bits and pieces, including replacement floorpans, often retaining the old chassis number to avoid new documentation, and, in some cases, tax. It is also difficult to check the authenticity of such vehicles because they were numbered in series with normal road-going 911s. The best solution is to call in expert help from one of the specialists.

It is perfectly practical, however, to build one of these cars from scratch, providing the price is not a deterrent. Only the detail fittings and some mechanical equipment is very much different from that of a normal 911.

CLUBS, SPECIALISTS & BOOKS

Clubs

Porsche clubs are very strong, which is hardly surprising considering the uncompromising nature of the cars. **The Porsche Club of Great Britain** is among the most enthusiastic, having been founded in 1961. From those early beginnings, it has evolved to provide an active social and competitive programme for members.

Each year, the club books an entire hotel for a weekend, in varying parts of the country. Drives are arranged through the surrounding countryside to see places of interest — and for members to surround themselves with the sound of Porsches! The weekend also features a dinner and dance, a film show, and a well-patronised bar for a noggin and a natter. Weekends abroad are also organised, with Guernsey as one location in 1982, and a visit to the factory in Stuttgart — for rather more than a weekend — as another regular occasion.

An annual club concours is held with a bring-and-buy parts sale, and there are workshop forums and instruction days organised throughout the country at the premises of Porsche specialists. Visits to police driving schools for instruction on the skid pans feature high on the list of useful attractions.

Race meetings are popular venues for club meetings, with support at most of the major events — in any case there is usually a Porsche of one form or another to support in endurance and other sports car events!

The club publishes a quarterly bulletin — *Porsche Post* — in order to unite the members who cannot otherwise participate in club events. There is no formal provision for spares or selling cars, but these services are available on an informed basis from other club members. Porsche's very comprehensive workshop manuals are kept for reference, however. **The Porsche Club of America** is one of the largest in the world, claiming 14,000 members. It publishes a monthly magazine called *Porsche Panorama,* carrying not only technical information on the practical side of owning a Porsche but advertising from specialists which is invaluable in view of the distances that can separate members. The Porsche Club of America is split into nearly one hundred chapters, which are, in effect, individual clubs. These cover the entire United States, including Hawaii. The national club organises attractions on a similar basis to those of the British club with a grand meeting in a holiday resort each year. As many as 600 cars turn up at such gatherings.

The executive director of the British club is Roy Gillham, of 64 Raisins Hill, Pinner, Middlesex (tel: London 866 7110) and the American club's address: 1753 Las Gallinas, San Rafael, CA 94903, USA (Tel: 415/472-0636, president Hank Malter). Additionally in the USA there is the **Porche Owners Club,** PO Box 54910, Terminal Annex, Los Angeles, CA 90054, USA (secretary Mark Rothman) and many smaller regional clubs.

Dotted around the world are so many Porsche clubs that it is impossible to list them here, however contact with any of the above clubs should yield a local address. There is a club in Germany dedicated to the Carrera RS only — **Club Porsche Carrera RS Interessingemeinschaft,** c/o Wilfried Holzenthal, Haupstrasse 36, 5419 Weidenhahn, W.Germany — Tel: 02666/776.

Specialists

Firms specialising in the 911 Carrera include: **Autofarm,** 5 Hill Avenue, Amersham, Bucks HP6 5BD, England (tel: 02403 21112); **AFN** — who also distribute new Porsches — 400 London Road, Isleworth, Middlesex TW7 5AG, England (tel: London 560 1011); **D.K. Engineering,** Whittles Yard, rear of 12-14 Hallowell Road, Northwood, Middlesex, England (tel: Northwood 21399/27012); **Charles Follett,** 6 Hall Road, St John's Wood, London NW8 9PA, England (tel: London 289 2211).

Books

Porsche has always been a very popular subject for specialist motoring books. For this reason it is not possible to list all the books that have been published on the marque. Instead, we give a list of the major titles currently available, in which there is special reference to the 911 Carrera.

The Porsche 911 (Chris Harvey, published by Oxford Illustrated Press/Haynes)
Porsches for the Road (Henry Rasmussen, published by Foulis/Haynes)
Porsche Double World Champions 1900-1977 (Richard von Frankenberg and Michael Cotton, published by Foulis/Haynes)
The Porsche 911 and derivatives (Michael Cotton, published by Motor Racing Publications)
The Porsche 911 Story (Paul Frere, published by Patrick Stephens)
Porsche — Excellence was Expected (Karl Ludvigsen. published by Automobile Quarterly)
The Great Marques — Porsche (Chris Harvey, published by Octopus)
The Porsche Book (Boschen and Barth, published by Patrick Stephens)

PHOTO GALLERY

1

1. The archetypal 911 Carrera: John Blatter's RS lightweight.

2

2. *The Carrera RS was originally fitted with Pirelli CN36 low-profile tyres on its old-style Porsche alloy wheels — but now it can be made to handle even better on Pirelli's latest offering, the P7.*

3. *The rear wheel arches of the Carrera RS bulged out slightly to cover the seven-inch rims and tyres.*

3

4

4. *The Carrera RS bore its 2.7 badge proudly on the engine lid — it used the first engine of that capacity in the Porsche range.*

5. *It's clear which is the most important information for the Porsche owner . . . the rev counter is in the centre of the instrument panel, flanked by the oil gauge and the speedometer.*

5

6

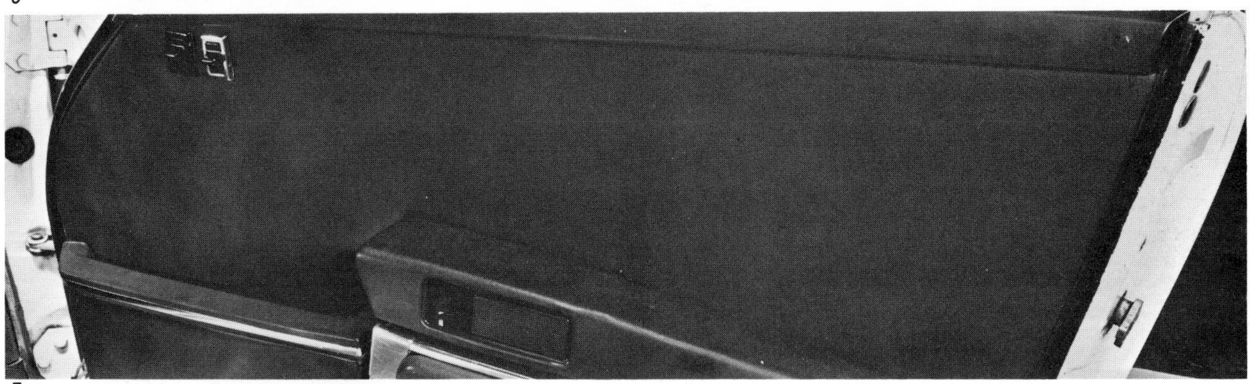

7

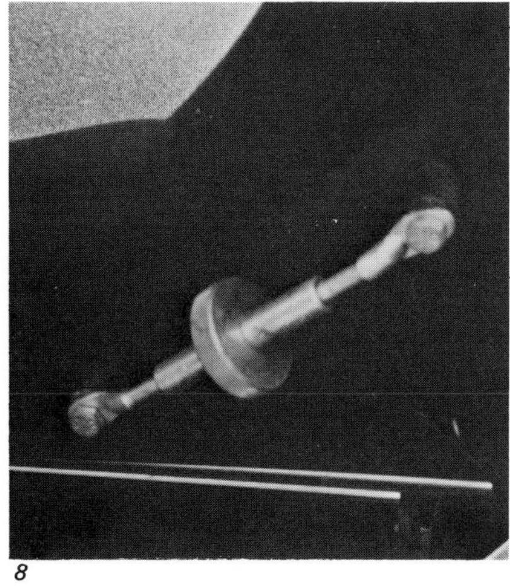

8

9

6. Despite the low roofline of the Carrera RS, the driver's view is high and wide.

7. RS lightweights had only a strap to work the door latch in the interests of weight-saving. The RS Touring door trim, pictured here, is the same as that of the 911S, with full trim and electric windows worked by the switches at the top left of the door's interior panel.

8. The RS lightweight was fitted with proper competition bucket seats complete with a massive alloy rake adjuster on the side.

9. There's no underseal to obscure the stark black-painted oil cooling lines along the underside of the sill on the RS lightweight.

10. The engine compartment of the RS lightweight is dominated by its 11-blade cooling fan on top of the cylinder blocks.

11. Deep down in the sides of the engine compartment of an RS lightweight, you'll find some spark plugs, beneath the fuel injection nozzles . . .

12. The engine installation of the G-series Carrera was little different from that of the RS lightweight.

13. Rear quarter view of the RS lightweight, showing its duck's tail spoiler. This example has been fitted with the more durable Touring steel over-riders and rubber bumper inserts.

10

12

11

13

14. The Carrera RS Touring differed little from the lightweight other than in trim, with carpet in places such as the luggage compartment.

15. When the carpet is removed from the front trunk of the Carrera RS Touring, the fuel tank is revealed. This car has been fitted with an oversize tank which means that a space-saver spare wheel has to be carried if luggage room is not to be sacrificed.

16 & 17. The RS Touring and later Carreras were fitted with two small rear seats as on other 911 models. These offered accommodation for two children, or one or two adults on short journeys, or, when folded flat, extra luggage on the platform created by their backs.

18. Porsche Carreras are full of thoughtful details for their owners, such as the luggage compartment light pictured here on this RS Touring model.

19. Careful attention should be paid to the cleanliness of a Carrera's alloy disc brake calipers to ensure that they do not seize through being soaked in a saline solution from salty winter roads. Disc ventilation slots can be clearly seen.

20. The sidelights, headlights and front bumper on the early Carreras were of outstandingly neat design.

14

15

16

17

18

19

20

21

22

23

24

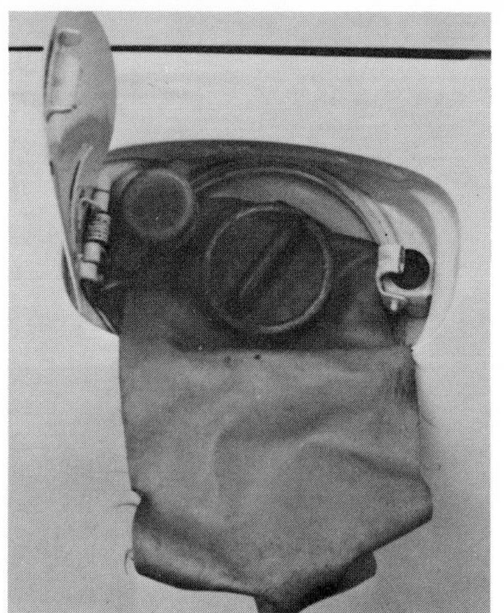

25

21 & 22. Two unusual views of a Porsche Carrera RS Touring — underneath the car, from the rear and from the front. These pictures emphasise the extremely clean underside profile of the 911 which contributes so much to its low drag factor and makes the car suitable for off-road use in rallies. In the first picture, the heat exchangers can be seen at the top flanking the crankcase and gearbox, and, in the second picture, the underside of the fuel tank can be seen at the top, between the front suspension arms, with the rear suspension 'bananas' at the bottom, linked by their anti-roll bar.

23. The interior of the G-series Carrera was revised with a padded steering wheel to meet new U.S. regulations in 1974. This car is fitted with a clock on the right of the panel because it is a Touring model.

24. Late in the G-series, the Carrera was fitted with a new 'picnic table' rubber-lipped spoiler at the back in place of the original 'duck's tail' design.

25. Porsche's attention to detail is legendary. Note how the Carrera's front wing fuel filler is fitted with a leather apron to protect the bodywork from accidental spillage.

26

26. The G-series Carrera in Targa form, showing its massive, built-in, roll hoop (finished in stainless steel on the earlier cars).

27. Three-quarter front view of the G-series Carrera showing the reinforced bumpers that followed the original lines so closely.

28. New seats with integral head restraints were introduced with the G-series Carrera.

29. The driver's exterior mirror on the Carrera 3 looks neatly streamlined and was compulsory in many countries but, unfortunately, took about 2mph off the top speed!

30. The door handles of the Carrera 3 were designed to present the safest possible profile.

27

28

29

30

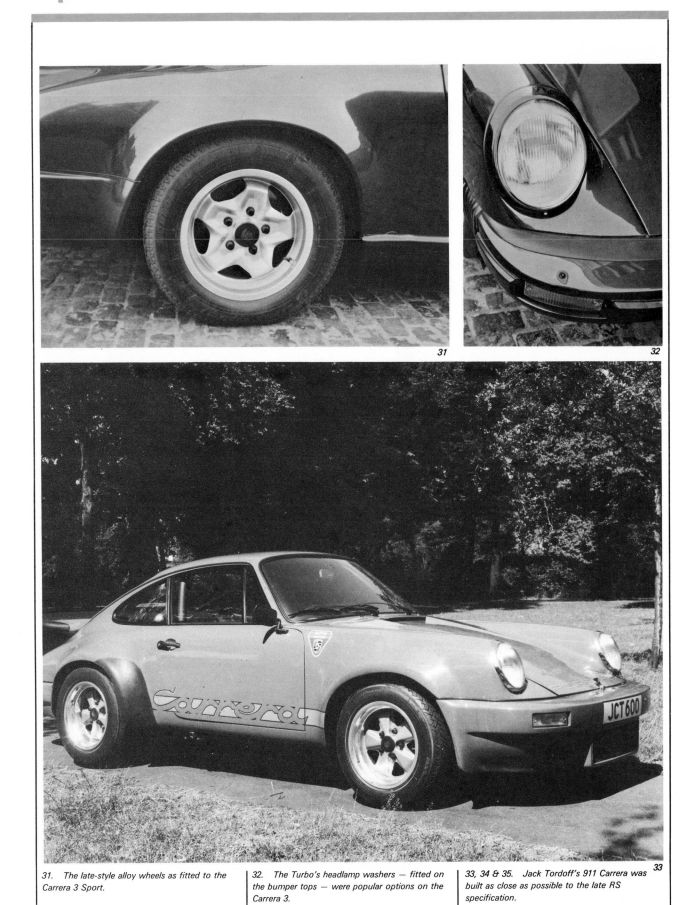

31. *The late-style alloy wheels as fitted to the Carrera 3 Sport.*

32. *The Turbo's headlamp washers — fitted on the bumper tops — were popular options on the Carrera 3.*

33, 34 & 35. *Jack Tordoff's 911 Carrera was built as close as possible to the late RS specification.*

34

35

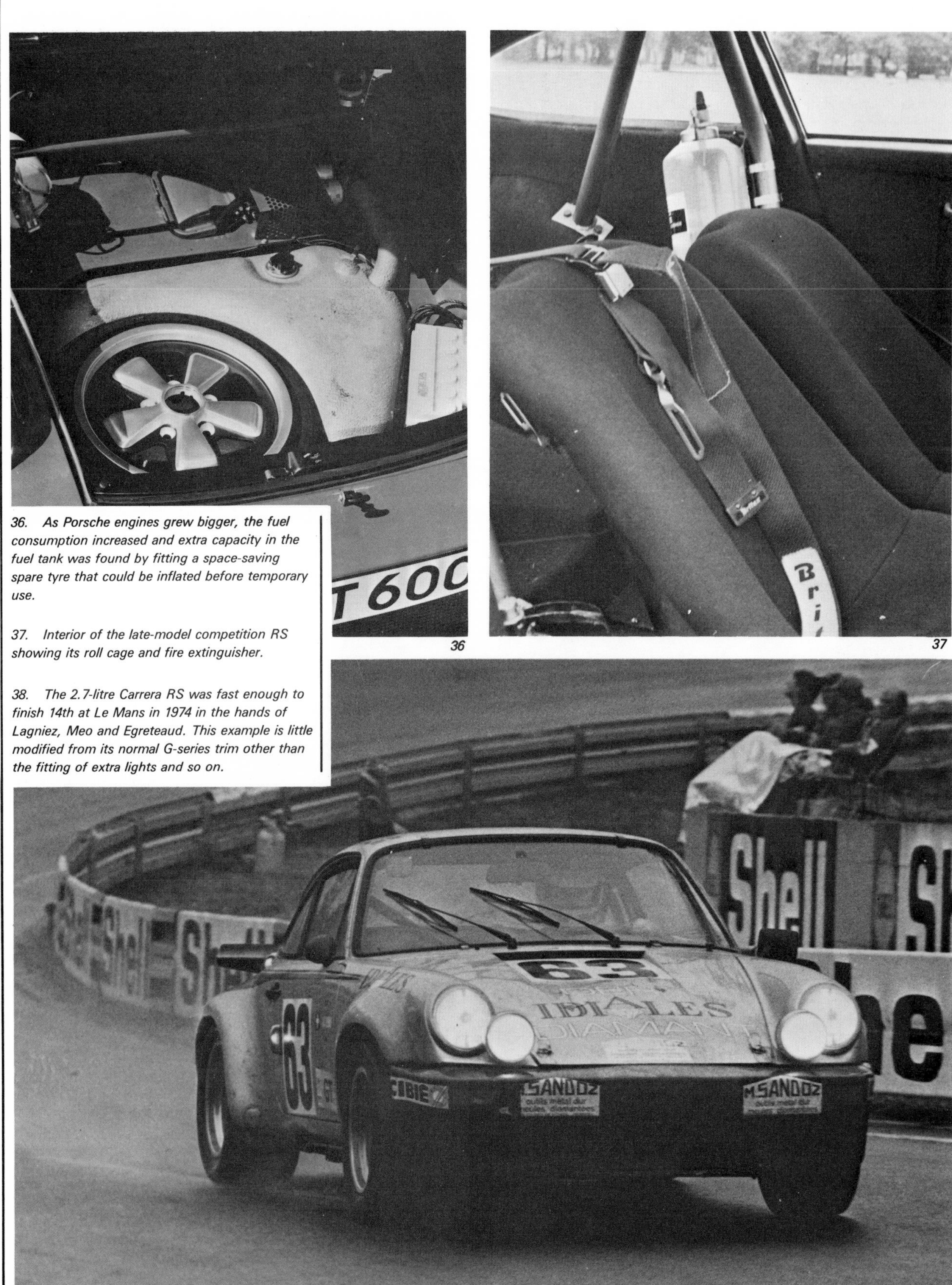

36. *As Porsche engines grew bigger, the fuel consumption increased and extra capacity in the fuel tank was found by fitting a space-saving spare tyre that could be inflated before temporary use.*

37. *Interior of the late-model competition RS showing its roll cage and fire extinguisher.*

38. *The 2.7-litre Carrera RS was fast enough to finish 14th at Le Mans in 1974 in the hands of Lagniez, Meo and Egreteaud. This example is little modified from its normal G-series trim other than the fitting of extra lights and so on.*

36

37

38

39, 40, 41 & 42. The Carrera RSR 3.0s were far faster at Le Mans in 1974, but these four examples, driven by Claude Ballot-Lena and Vic Elford (number 61), Strieberg, Kirschoffer and Chateau (number 60), Georg Loos, Clemens Schickentanz and Jurgen Barth (number 64), and Claude Haldi, Jose-Maria Fernandez and Jean-Marc Sequin, all retired.

39

40

41

42

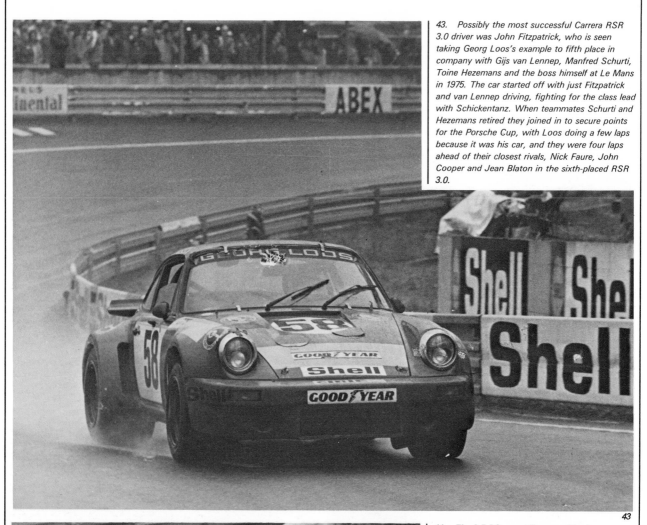

43. Possibly the most successful Carrera RSR 3.0 driver was John Fitzpatrick, who is seen taking Georg Loos's example to fifth place in company with Gijs van Lennep, Manfred Schurti, Toine Hezemans and the boss himself at Le Mans in 1975. The car started off with just Fitzpatrick and van Lennep driving, fighting for the class lead with Schickentanz. When teammates Schurti and Hezemans retired they joined in to secure points for the Porsche Cup, with Loos doing a few laps because it was his car, and they were four laps ahead of their closest rivals, Nick Faure, John Cooper and Jean Blaton in the sixth-placed RSR 3.0.

43

44. The 2.7 RS was still competitive in endurance racing in 1975, this example, driven by Joel Laplacette, Claude Pigeon and Alain Leroux competing at Le Mans.

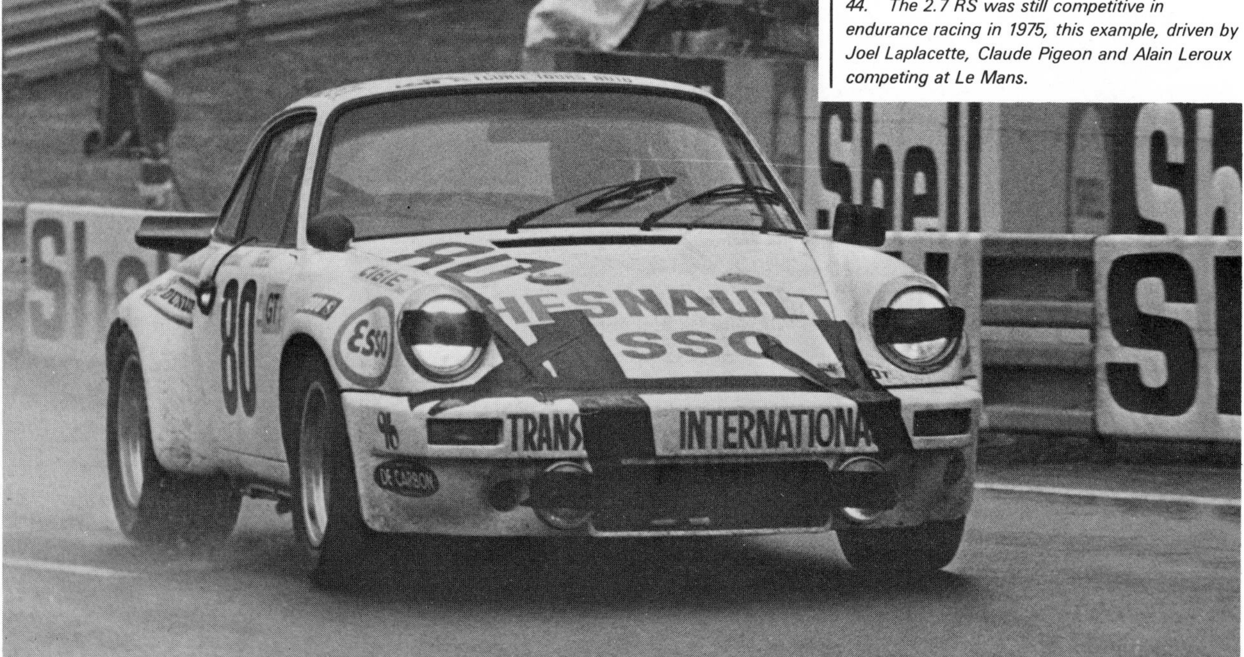

44

45

45. The Mexicans Hector Rebaque and Memo Rojas, with Belgian Freddie van Beuren, took over Peter Gregg and Hurley Haywood's 1975 Daytona-winning RSR 3.0, fitting it with a three-litre turbocharged engine from a Porsche 934 for Le Mans in 1976. They qualified in 39th place before retiring with a broken distributor. This ex-works car, with its extra-wide rear track and RSR Turbo-style wing, had to race as a prototype. Note the U.S.-style quick-release windscreen catches normally used in IMSA GT racing.

46

46. The Carrera RS was one of the most popular top-line cars in rallying in the mid-1970s, particularly in tarmac events such as the Galway International Rally. The fastest and most spectacular of 12 Carreras in this event was driven by Jan Churchill and Rupert Saunders. Their famous yellow car is seen here, with its rear end crumpled, on the fourth special stage. It stormed on despite broken engine mountings with the power unit held in chiefly by its sump guard! Later, Churchill secured the engine with a bit from a pneumatic drill to challenge the winner, Billy Coleman in a Ford Escort RS1800, on several stages before having to retire when flames blowing back from a split exhaust melted the carburettor air intakes. Ken Shields led in the Carrera contingent with a second place.

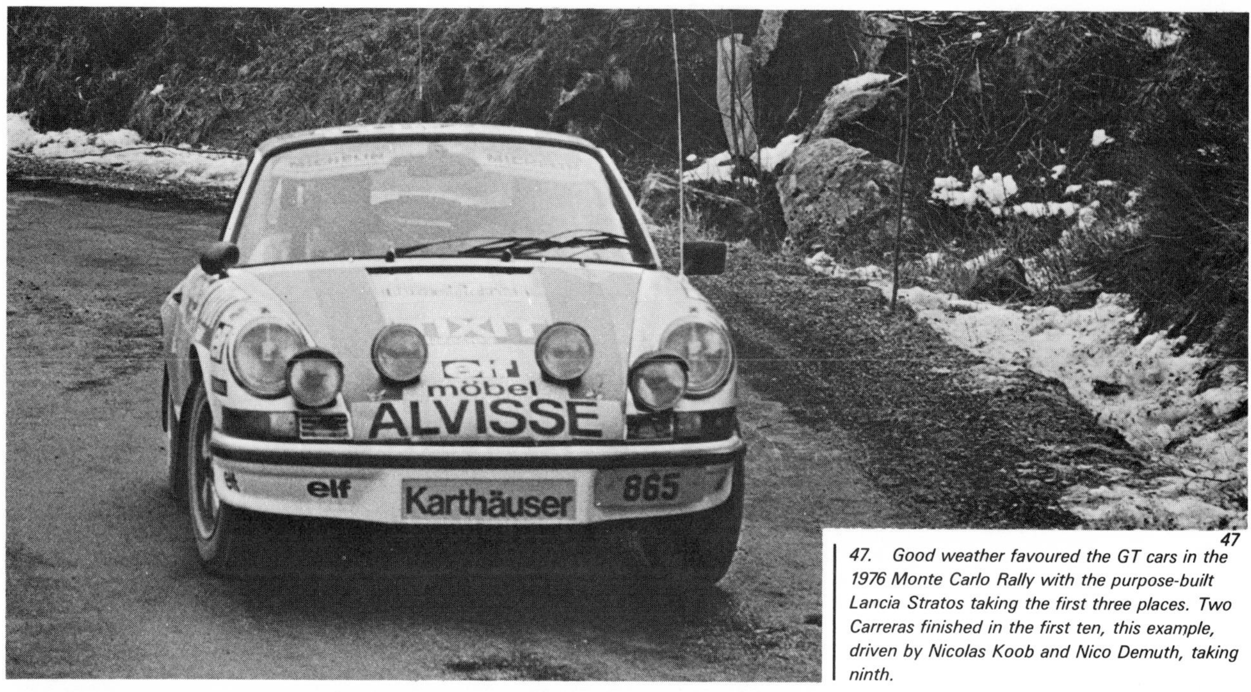

47

47. *Good weather favoured the GT cars in the 1976 Monte Carlo Rally with the purpose-built Lancia Stratos taking the first three places. Two Carreras finished in the first ten, this example, driven by Nicolas Koob and Nico Demuth, taking ninth.*

48

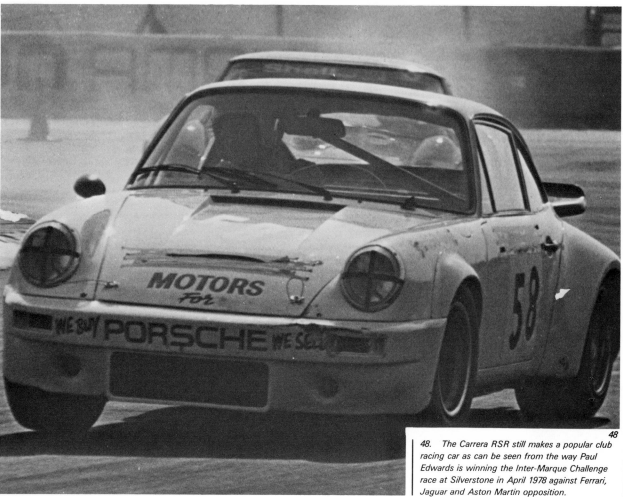

48. *The Carrera RSR still makes a popular club racing car as can be seen from the way Paul Edwards is winning the Inter-Marque Challenge race at Silverstone in April 1978 against Ferrari, Jaguar and Aston Martin opposition.*

49

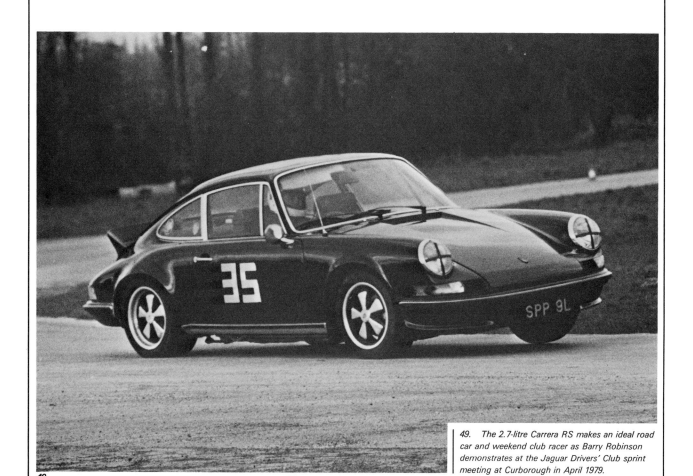

49. The 2.7-litre Carrera RS makes an ideal road car and weekend club racer as Barry Robinson demonstrates at the Jaguar Drivers' Club sprint meeting at Curborough in April 1979.

50

50. Weekend racer extraordinary ... the 3.0 RSR of Dudley Woods and Barrie Williams takes tenth place in the World Championship of makes six-hour race at Brands Hatch in August 1979. It is seen here leading the very similar, but rather younger, 2.8-litre 911SC of Jean-Louis Schlesser, Gerard Bleynie and Jacques Guerrin, which finished 13th.

51

52

51. Barry Robinson and Paul Edwards combined with Richard Cleare to drive the Edwards RSR into 21st place in the Brands Hatch six-hour in August 1979.

52 & 53. Close cousin of the RSR, the 934 of Georges Bourdillat, Pascal Ennequin and Gerard Vial finished 19th in the 1979 Brands Hatch six-hour.

53

54

55

54. Lloyd Evans and Laurie Ritchie are seen sharing a late Carrera RS at the Midland Hillclimb Championship at Prescott in April 1982.

55. Classic cornering from John Lowe's 2.8-litre Targa at Prescott in April 1982.

56. *Even standard road-going Porsche Carreras — in this case Tim Milvain's 2.7-litre model complete with spotlight nacelles and sunroof — make good hillclimb cars. Tim is pictured here at Ettore's Bend at Prescott in April 1982.*

57. *Porsche's heritage stretches back to the mountains of Austria, and they have lost nothing on the way, as can be seen from the way Larry Hirst's 2.7-litre Carrera Targa — showing an early combination of G-series body and 'duck's tail' spoiler — handled at Prescott in April 1982. For the uninitiated, the vertical black bar ahead of the front bumper cuts the electronic timing beams at the start and conclusion of the climb.*

C1

C2

C3

C1. The classic Carrera RS lightweight in its original paint and trim.

C2. The distinctive duck's tail spoiler and lettering as used on the early Carrera RS.

C3. The centres of the alloy wheels on the early Carrera RS cars were finished in blue, red or green, with the bodywork usually in white. These tyres are of lower profile than the originals.

C4

C4. Everything possible was done to save weight on the Carrera RS, even to the extent of painting on the model and maker's name, rather than fitting chrome badges. It started a trend with other sporting cars . . . Note the widened arches of the RS. The steel over-riders of this car are non-original.

C5. Hunched and ready to go, the Carrera RS lightweight hugs the ground . . .

C5

C6

C7

C8.

C6, C7 & C8. These cameos of an early Carrera RS Touring show how little it differs from the original lightweight upon which it is based. From any angle the car has a purposeful, but smooth shape and is in remarkably good, original condition.

C9. The 'picnic table', rubber-edged spoiler of this G-series model was designed to provide the best possible aerodynamics without projecting beyond the car's plan form or interfering with the engine's air intake.

C10. The G-series was much revised, with the Carrera name being transferred to the top-of-the-line normal road cars. It also meant that the Targa top became available on a Carrera . . . this has to be one of the nicest ways to go open air motoring.

C11. White is a traditional Porsche colour which seems to compliment the basic 911 shape. This G-series model illustrates just how well Porsche were able to integrate the impact absorbing bumpers, demanded by American law, into the 911 design. With the softening of the Carrera theme, the G-series brought luxuries like the side rubbing strips of this Targa.

C9

C10

C11

C12

C13

C12. Porsche Carreras stand out in a crowd . . . particularly when finished in brilliant red.

C13. The Carrera 3 complete with handy accessories, such as spotlights, headlamp washers, and driver's exterior mirror.

C 14

C15

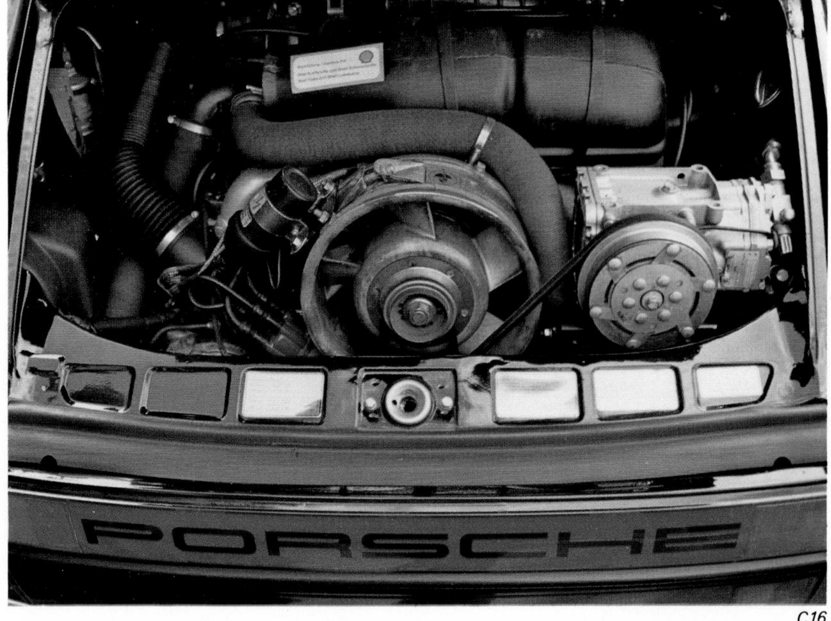

C16

C14. Another view of the very fully equipped Carrera 3 — a very desirable car!

C15. Close-up of the wheels, bumper and spoiler of the Carrera 3.

C16. Engine room of the Carrera 3, with its later five-bladed fan. The massive pump on the right of the bay is for the optional air-conditioning . . . a far cry from the original lightweight and its spartan specification!

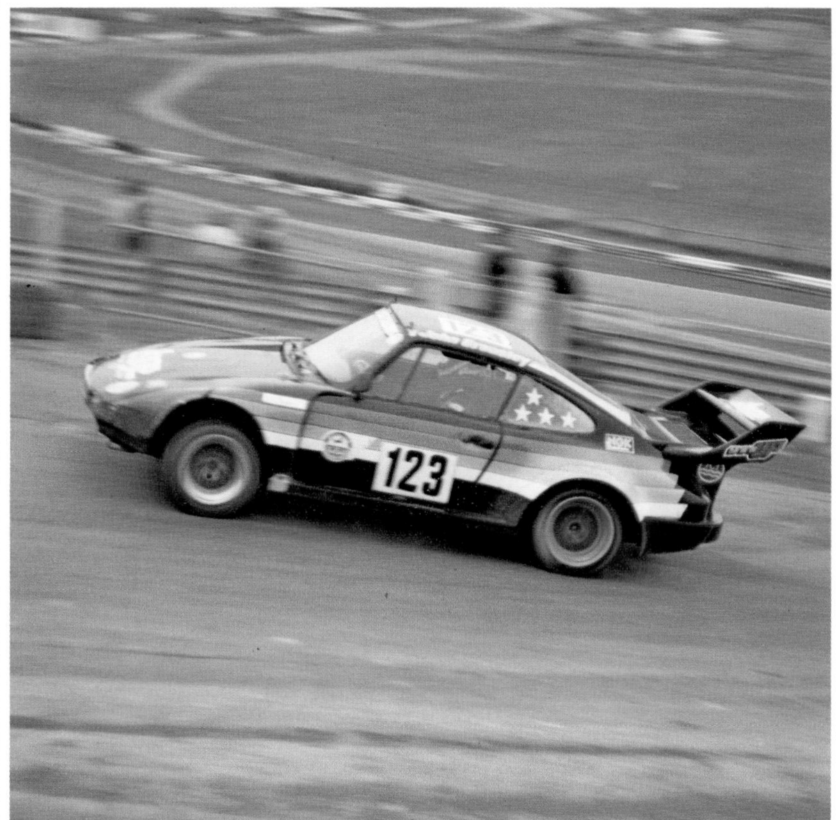

C17

C17. John Harper and John Beasley drove the BAT Motors Carrera RSR into 11th place in the 1979 Brands Hatch Six-Hour.

C18. One of the most consistent competitors in Rallycross, John Greasley, was out of luck with his 3.3-litre Carrera, attacking the barriers twice in the slippery Lloyds and Scottish round at Brands Hatch in January 1982.

C18.

C19. One of Britain's most formidable competitors in hillclimbing, John Sadler — a partner in Autofarm — storms to a class win at Prescott in April 1982. His car is the ultimate road-going Carrera, fitted with a 3506cc engine built up with extra large bore and stroke. Josh set a time of 47.57 sec, his record standing at 46.42.

C20. Tim Milvain's immaculate 2.7-litre road Carrera sweeps up Prescott in April 1982.

C19

C20